IF HE CAN DO IT,
I CAN DO IT

Published by Hurdling Handicaps
P.O. Box 725023
Berkley, MI 48072
www.hurdlinghandicaps.org

Publisher's Cataloging-in-Publication Data
Patton, Larry.

If he can do it, I can do it : the inspiring story of Larry Patton living beyond his disability / by Larry Patton with Diane S. Wyss. — Berkley, MI : Hurdling Handicaps, 2005.

p. ; cm.
ISBN: 0-9770647-0-0
ISBN 13: 978-0-9770647-0-0

1. Patton, Larry. 2. Cerebral palsied-Biography. 3. People with disabilities-Biography. I. Wyss, Diane S. II. Title.

RC388 .P38 2005
616.8/36-dc22   2005932985

Project coordination by Jenkins Group, Inc. • www.bookpublishing.com
Cover design by Christian Fuenfhausen
Interior design by Cecile Kaufman

Printed in the United States of America
09 08 07 06 05 • 5 4 3 2 1

Dedications

FROM LARRY:

To Jennifer, my wife. Thank you for all the love, encouragement, and support you have given me throughout our marriage and for being my best friend and a wonderful mother to our children.

To Will and Anna, my children. What a wonderful gift and blessing you are from the Lord!

To Bill and Sue Patton, my parents. Thank you for showing me the love of Christ through your daily Christian walk. Thank you for assisting me in building a firm Christian foundation to build my life upon and for instilling an "I can do it with Christ" attitude in me.

FROM DIANE:

To James G. Wyss, my husband. You taught me to use the talents the Lord has given me. Thank you for your unconditional love, encouragement, and blessings over the past twenty-two years of marriage. Thank you for being a loving and dedicated father to our children. You give and lead selflessly with God's grace. I love you!

To my children, Jimmy, Benjamin, Sarah, Amy, Samuel, Melissa, and Joel Wyss. I love you all! Each of you shall continue to be my inspiration! I love the joy you bring into my life. Each of you is truly a unique blessing from the Lord!

"Her children arise and call her blessed . . . "

PROVERBS 31:28

Contents

Acknowledgments

We wish to thank the following people for their help in making this book possible. First, thank you to our Lord and Savior for using us in ways we never dreamed possible!

Thanks to Harry Krupsky, for your time and for writing the forward; to James L. and Joan Wyss, Bob and Kate Nyquist, and Greg Doozan, for inspiring insights and details; to Diane Lipinski, for reading the manuscript in raw form; to Christa Shewe, for your valuable advise; to Gerry Santoro, for descriptive details; to Trina Masanery, for inspiring the title for this book, to Val Doozan, Mike and Kathy Bauss, and Rick Lipinski, for your special encouragement and prayers; to Linda Arms, for your encouragement; and to Bob Santoro, for valuable art advice and help.

We also need to thank Jimmy Wyss for being our walking thesaurus, Ben Wyss for ideas, Sarah Wyss for poetry help and ideas, Amy Wyss for art consultations, Sam Wyss for ideas and humor, and Melissa and Joel Wyss for bringing food, water, and hugs and kisses.

Thank you also to Jenny Patton, for reading the rough draft and using your red pen. Thanks also for all the hours of interviews and for believing in this project.

James G. Wyss, you sure can wield a mean shop vac. You gave technical support and encouragement and you believed in this project from the beginning. Thank you.

Finally, thank you to the many people who believed this project could happen and prayed this book into existence.

All scripture references are taken from the New International Version of the Bible.

Some of the names and events have been changed to protect the privacy of certain individuals.

Foreword

If He Can Do It, I Can Do It . . . Having shared life and ministry with Larry for the past eight years, I cannot imagine a better title for a book about his life. In the years I have known Larry, the Lord has used him to inspire thousands of people to go beyond their own handicaps.

I remember the first time I heard Larry say, "We all have handicaps . . . some are just more visible to other people." His words touched my heart in a very personal way. Not in a way that led to self-pity, but rather in a way that helped me to accept who I am and, with God's help, to become all that I can possibly be.

As inspirational as Larry's life story is, the true legacy he leaves with all who know him is one of faith in Jesus Christ. Whether he is golfing, snow skiing, public speaking, serving as Men's Ministry director, or being a husband, father, or friend, Larry's inspiration, his source of strength and vision, comes from his faith relationship in his Lord and Savior Jesus Christ.

Any of us who know Larry know the title of his book comes from his personal inspiration, God's Word, when it says, "I can do everything through Him who gives me strength" (Philippians 4:13).

I know that Larry's deepest desire is that God's Spirit will use this story of his life to point every person to the one story that changes a person's eternity, the story of Jesus Christ.

Harry Krupsky
Minister of Family Life
Faith Lutheran Church
Troy, Michigan

"*Trust in the LORD with all of your heart
and lean not on your own understanding;
in all your ways acknowledge him,
and he will make your paths straight.*"
PROVERBS 3:5,6

"*I believe that God is in me as the sun is in
the color and fragrance of a flower . . . the light
in my darkness, the Voice in my Silence.*"
HELEN KELLER

Prologue

*I*t was already dark. The Michigan wind blew hard, sending a chill through the crowd of people waiting. The misting rain changed to sleet, and January 6, 2002, turned into an extra-ordinary evening in the southeastern part of the state.

As the crowd huddled at Woodward Avenue and the Davison Exchange, a voice boomed out, "Here he comes!"

An onlooker quickly bowed her head and uttered a quiet prayer. "Please Lord, don't let him fall!"

Off in the distance a flickering light moved forward, growing bigger and brighter, bobbing up and down as it moved closer.

"Please Lord, make his feet steady; keep him strong!" the same spectator prayed.

Cheers erupted from the crowd as he passed by with the flame. "You can do it! Go Larry, go! Go Larry, go! Go Larry, go!" Over and over the crowd chanted a continuous rhythm of cheers and encouragement.

The Olympic Flame burned especially bright that evening as Larry Patton carried it two-tenths of a mile, while running remarkably smoothly. This was a most difficult task for Larry. During his birth, complications had caused oxygen deprivation resulting in cerebral palsy, with life-long effects.

Larry, with physical limitations in a twisted body, was a significant visual picture for all that cold January night. His strength in overcoming his disability was inspirational to those who caught a glimpse of him. His example told everyone, no matter what hindrance might lie in their path, it would not be too difficult to overcome with God's help. The crowd came to encourage Larry that night, but he in turn served as the encourager.

"Lord, let them see you here right now as I run with this lighted torch. Let people be drawn to You. Let them know You are the Light of the world. Help me walk and not grow weary, to run and not grow faint; Lord, mount me up as on the wings of an eagle," was his prayer that night. It was a prayer that had shaped his entire life.

The people who gathered to watch the Olympic Flame pass by caught an unexpected piece of truth that evening as they watched this man run: everyone is in some way handicapped, be it physically, emotionally, or spiritually.

Larry ran with a burning light of hope and anticipation, and much more than the Olympic spirit was present that night. The spirit of Almighty God used Larry Patton in a disabled body full of frustrating limitations to expose our limitations and give us hope that goes beyond ourselves.

Yes, the Olympic Torch burned brightly in Detroit for an evening, but the Spirit of the Living God burns forever in the hearts of those who are drawn to receive him.

The Olympic Flame carried by Larry Patton was passed to another runner waiting his turn, thus leaving Larry's torch extinguished, but the Living God promises, "I will not crush the bruised reed, nor will I put out the smoldering wick" (Isaiah 42:3).

Unlike any earthly light, He is alive, bringing hope and salvation, and making exquisite beauty out of broken lives.

IF HE CAN DO IT,
I CAN DO IT

"But those who
hope in the LORD
will renew their STRENGTH.
They will SOAR on
wings like eagles;
they will RUN and
not grow weary,
they will WALK
and not be faint."

Isaiah 40:31

1

Learning to Fly on the Wings of an Eagle

✳

"Even youths grow tired and weary, and young men stumble and fall; but those who hope in the LORD will renew their strength. They will soar on wings like eagles; they will run and not grow weary, they will walk and not be faint."

Isaiah 40: 30, 31

I stood in the kitchen of my beautiful, fully furnished San Jose apartment, stunned. I was very tired and hungry after working late and could not bring myself to eat another meal in a restaurant. I just wanted something to eat from home—my home.

"Just a quick peanut butter and jelly sandwich will hit the spot and hold me over so I can cook a homemade meal," I thought. Holding my right hand steady with my left, I managed to get peanut butter onto one piece of bread, and in the same fashion started with the jelly onto the other piece of bread. Though I was successfully employed by IBM and managing my disability needs independently, I was used to simple tasks such as this giving me a challenge.

In 1958, when I was two years old, I was diagnosed with cerebral palsy (cp). The classification my cp fell into was Athetoid. This classification is characterized by nerve damage and muscle contractures. As a result, my brain cannot send proper signals through my nervous system, which means I have random, uncontrollable, jerky movements in my extremities and body.

The nerves and muscles in my tongue are also affected, making articulation and speech difficult and hard to understand.

Doing basic everyday tasks has always presented a challenge for me, things such as getting dressed, walking, speaking, and eating. It may take me several minutes to put on a shirt, whereas the average person can slip on a shirt without thinking about it. When I stand up, my legs and feet turn inward, making even simple walking a challenge. Eating demands much effort. The unsteady movements of my arms can make getting food into my mouth a struggle, and I always drink liquids through a straw.

Making a PB&J seemed to be a task I could manage, until I picked up that contoured glass jar of jelly. I was trying to time the uncontrollable rolling movements of my arms with getting the jelly to land on the bread. Just when I thought I had gotten the jelly to the edge of the jar using a knife, the glass jar slipped from my hand and, in what seemed to be slow motion, hit the counter and then came smashing down onto the floor. I stood over the mess and just stared at the broken glass mixed with sticky jelly that spread across the kitchen floor, managing to splash up onto the lower cupboard doors as well.

"What a mess!" I thought. I was glad I hadn't changed out of my nice work clothes into shorts, because the long pants and dress shoes kept the glass off my legs and feet. "This would be a good time to call Mom and Dad, but I doubt they would come all the way to California to clean up this mess for me."

The various sizes of glass that lay shattered on the floor posed a significant threat to me. With my random, uncontrolled movements, I couldn't risk cutting my hands. As I stood over the mess, wondering what to do next, my thoughts traveled back to just a month and a half ago, when I'd stepped out to take this challenge. I thought specifically about the morning I'd left my home in Michigan for California.

Tension had hung in the air as we drove to the airport. Ambivalence seemed to be my new companion while we waited in the sterile terminal. I didn't want Mom and Dad to know the extent of how I was feeling, so I did my best not to show my emotions. I knew Mom was very worried for me.

I hugged Mom as she wiped tears from her eyes, and as Dad gave me a strong handshake, he kept his tears from falling, as if to not let on about his concern for me.

I still remember Steve, my younger brother, simply saying, "Larry, have a fun time."

I hugged Steve one last time.

The flight attendant at the desk asked, "Sir, would you like a wheelchair?"

"No thank you," I replied. "I don't think I'll be needing one." I turned to wave one last time, then started to board the plane early to be out of the way of the other travelers on the flight. On that hot, steamy morning of August 4, 1979, I walked down the hall out of my family's sight and onto a plane headed for California.

I was filled with strange excitement, anticipating the thrill of the new challenge that lured me forward, but at the same time afraid of the unknown obstacles I knew I would soon encounter.

This whole move came as a surprise. When I was hired into IBM, I never considered the possibility of traveling, let alone moving across the country. When I reported for my first full day of work in the Detroit office, my boss told me I needed to go to California for a three- to six-month stint to learn more about the research and development (R&D) end of IBM. "It'll round out your job responsibilities," he told me. "You have what we think we need."

I had only a few short weeks to prepare for my move. My boss was gracious enough to let me have an extra week to tie up loose ends, which allowed me to go on the trip I had planned for the youth group at church and to attend my good friend's wedding.

The long ramp led me into the plane, much like cattle being led into a pen. I was on my own now, and I felt nervous. In fact, I was scared to death! I proceeded down the aisle to find my seat. I used the task of searching carefully for my place to ease the feeling of leaving Mom, Dad, and Steve behind.

I reasoned with myself, saying, "I have to do this . . . I have to go where IBM sends me . . . I hope I can learn everything IBM wants me to," but my logic didn't remove the lonely and uncertain feelings lurking inside.

While the plane started down the runway, I noticed how full this flight was. Who were all of these people and where were they going? Finally the plane was airborne and I was really on my way to California. I was glad to have a seat next to the window because I was looking forward to the view. "Looking down at the awesome creation God made might serve as a distraction for me," I thought.

Seeing the landscape grow smaller and smaller, I was reminded of how small I felt at that moment. I turned my attention to the other passengers in the plane, most of them busy reading or working, lost in their own worlds. They seemed to know what was waiting for them. I refocused my gaze out the window, wondering when I would feel sure and certain of my world again.

Arrival in San Jose, California, came after many hours of traveling and a long layover in Denver. Upon making my connecting flight, I was thankful to have an aisle seat so I could stretch my stiff, twisted legs. Being completely exhausted from travel made getting up from my seat on the plane difficult once we landed outside of San Jose. I sat for just a moment trying to gather my thoughts concerning the details that lay ahead of me that afternoon.

My thoughts were suddenly interrupted. "Excuse me," said the large, middle-aged man who was seated next to the window.

With a slight irritation in his voice that he accentuated with hand motions, he announced, "I need to get past."

With fatigue dictating my body, I stood up as quickly as I could manage. The man, seeing my disability, gave me a half-hearted "Thank you" as he heaved a sigh and brushed past me.

The last one to exit the plane, I grabbed my belongings and trudged down the plane's narrow aisle, heading toward the gate.

My next step was to look for my new connection, an employee holding an IBM sign at the gate. "God, what am I doing?" My mind demanded answers. "Will this person know whom to look for? Will anyone be here waiting for me? I know absolutely no one here!" When I didn't get any answers to my confused questions, I resorted to prayer instead. "Please Lord, work this out for me."

I had been so excited when I hired on at IBM, but now I was beginning to doubt my ability to perform as this job required "I need to keep pressing forward to do my best," I said, trying to coach myself. "No! What I really need is to do better than my best, alleviating any doubts or concerns about my disability in the minds of my superiors. Can I make a solid impression doing research and development?" The questions came and went, always haunting and leaving me filled with anxiety.

Two years into my college career at Wayne State University in Detroit, Michigan, I had started a training program at IBM through Vocational Rehabilitation where I gained valuable professional experience. Now, after graduation, I was a full-time employee.

"Lord, did I take a bigger step than I can handle trying to tackle R&D? Not only am I shouldering a whole new job description, I will be living far from home with my disability for the first time." I felt heavy with anxiety and fear, now wondering how long I would journey with this weight on me. Again, more questions, and more concerns to consume me.

Back home in Michigan, I lived just a few short blocks from Mom and Dad's house. I knew I could always pick up the phone and Mom or Dad would be there in a matter of minutes. This move was going to require a trust in God that I wasn't sure I had.

Without question I overworked my imagination, which in turn gave my emotions control over me. With this in mind, as one would guess, I met my IBM contact at the gate without incident. Barry, my contact, took me to a car rental agency. After thanking him, I managed the details of getting the car, but now came the real problem: I had to drive the streets in the Southern Bay area.

Believe it or not, when I was sixteen, in spite of the Athetoid movements, I passed my driving exam and was granted a Michigan driver's license. But here in California, with the traffic strange to me and not knowing my way, I felt very anxious about this drive to the Holiday Inn where my reservation was waiting.

After searching a map in my rented late '70s model Grand Am, I was on my way once again, driving through a surprisingly nice scenic stretch of the Bay area. The palm trees were beautiful, the breeze was warm and dry, and the ride seemed to keep unfolding more beauty as I continued winding around the hills on the nearly empty roads. For the first time that day, despite not knowing exactly where I was going, I felt a calm wash over me as I took in the strange new beauty of my surroundings.

"This is not like Michigan," I mused, feeling a sense of excitement beginning to build again. The new territory to discover was filling me with curiosity, and I knew it wouldn't be long before I'd be out there amongst the natural wonders that were beckoning me to experience them.

As I traveled the highway, I noticed a sign that gave directions to the IBM building I was to report to the next morning. At that moment, reality reminded me that I was not there to explore for a living. I could feel my body tighten slightly as I thought about my first day on the job in the California office.

"It's okay," I assured myself. "I trusted God this far; I can do it tomorrow as well." I was naïve to what trust meant at this point in the experience, but I did know that God was with me so far, and that He was trustworthy in keeping his promise to watch over me.

The next day announced its arrival as the bright yellow sunlight splashed through the gaps in the hotel curtains. I struggled to sit up in bed. Rubbing my eyes, I focused on the alarm clock. 7:15 a.m. Panic filled me. "I over slept forty-five minutes! Being late is not the way to make a good first impression!"

I was to be in the office by 8:00 a.m. As I rushed about getting ready, I calculated how long it would take me to get there. It was a fifteen-minute ride from the hotel, so I put myself in high gear, fastening my Velcro-altered, button-up white shirt and clipping on my blue striped tie to be ready on time for my big day, my new beginning.

Before I had left for California, my mother had converted all my button-up shirts to close with Velcro, keeping the buttons on the outside so the shirts would still look like regular shirts. This was a fantastic help for me because I did not have the fine motor skills for tasks such as buttoning my shirt.

While driving to my new office, I thought about how quickly my life had changed. Here I was, twenty-three years old, terrified of the prospect ahead, doubting my abilities, and wondering why I was about to step into the place that had brought me clear across the country.

I could not have known then that opening the door and stepping into the IBM world would make a significant change in my life and in the lives of others. Each day brought challenges, and I managed them one by one. Though a few people around me were not comfortable with my disability, which caused them to overlook my ability to perform on the job, I persevered and proved to myself and my superiors that I did indeed have what IBM needed.

I remember the first presentation I had to do. Several individuals put me to the test, but this pressure was just the thing to make me try harder. Slowly the days turned into weeks, and my skills made it clear that I was capable of taking on the tasks of R&D.

A couple of weeks went by, and I became weary of living out of a suitcase. It was now time to find a place to call home. I found an apartment about eight miles from the office and it was great, fully furnished, with a balcony, and completely up-dated in the latest 1970's décor.

I felt like I had it all. Not only was my apartment awesome, but the location was as well. The ocean was a forty-five minute drive to the west, and in the opposite direction, another forty minutes led me right to the mountains.

Yes, I was now ready to take in and enjoy California. After growing up in Michigan, with its many changes in seasons and weather, I found it fascinating that the trees never lost their leaves and it seldom rained here.

After being in my apartment for a couple of weeks, I was able to lease a new car. From then on, every Friday after work I would gas up my 1979, Z-28 rust-colored Camero. I would find a destination on the map by closing my eyes and touching the map—wherever my finger landed, that was where I headed. The weather seemed to always be in the mid-seventies, providing the perfect scenario for driving with the windows down, letting the warm breeze rush against my face.

I spent those hours talking with the Lord. "This is so good," I would utter while starting up the engine of my awesome new car. I felt my independence and my confidence building daily.

To enhance this feeling of confidence, I was drawing a substantial paycheck for the first time in my life. I would send money home to Mom and Dad, pay my bills, and enjoy life a little more than I had in the past. This was a time in my life that I will always look back on with memories of change, growth, and deep inner satisfaction.

I had been terribly nervous going across the country, not knowing another soul, but God made provisions for me at work.

One man in particular was a blessing. Dick, his wife Judy, and their four children opened their home to me by inviting me to dinner several nights a week. I found my California church home through them.

Before long, I met several friends at work and at church who took turns going to the beach or sightseeing with me every weekend. If we went to the beach, Frisbees and a picnic dinner were essentials. There was nothing more enjoyable than playing Frisbee with my new friends on the warm beaches of California.

Throwing a Frisbee back and forth was a great way for me to get exercise, and the sand made a soft landing when I fell down trying to catch the flying disk. It was white and clean, the ocean breeze was filled with the scent of saltwater, and the tide pools held captive pieces of kelp and ocean weeds that washed in from the tide.

"What carefree days these are," I would tell my friends as we packed up for a day at the beach. My life up to this point had always been focused on making a way for my disability in this world. I felt very accepted by my new friends and I could see God watching over me through the network of Christian fellowship. Without realizing it, the anxieties I had come to California with slowly melted away one by one.

✳

As these thoughts and memories faded I became reacquainted with the sticky jelly mess waiting on my floor. I asked myself out loud, "How am I going to get this cleaned up?" I'm not sure if I really expected an answer, but in an instant Scott came to mind.

"Perhaps if I call him, he would come over to help," I thought. "It's worth a try." I won't ask just anyone for help, because I can sense within a few minutes of being in someone's presence how comfortable they are with my disability. Shuffling around the glass shards to the phone on the kitchen wall, I remembered why I had such confidence in Scott.

I got to know my co-worker while working late one evening at the office. It was going on 8:00 p.m., and when my stomach growled, I realized I hadn't eaten since breakfast that morning. I was enjoying my work, and it wasn't uncommon for me to get so engrossed that I worked right through lunch or past supper.

To get to the facility cafeteria, I had to pass Scott's office. He was in there finishing up a few details concerning his day's work. I'd met him briefly when I was first introduced to members connected to R&D in my corner of the building; he'd seemed like an unassuming, compassionate fellow who enjoyed being around people.

On this particular evening, I decided to take a chance. I stopped at his lighted office, with its always-welcoming open door, and took the opportunity to peak my head in, asking, "You want to get a bite to eat?"

"Hey, Larry! I'd love to!" was his response. That was the beginning of a great relationship with a great friend that has lasted over the years. As we sat across from each other, me with my BBQ beef sandwich and Scott with his tuna salad, we shared our stories about how we'd come to work at IBM.

After a while into the conversation, Scott's heart grew heavy and sad. I studied his face as he spoke. Behind his large, dark-rimmed glasses, I saw his eyes fill with tears. He stopped for a moment to regain composure, pushed his dark curly hair off to the right, then began again. He and his wife were separating, and though in some ways it seemed like a good idea, it would not take away the ache inside of Scott for the love of his wife of eight years and their three daughters.

Scott was living in a house alone, only three miles from my apartment, so I hoped he would be available to help with my predicament. I called him to explain my situation and immediately he responded by saying, "Larry, I will be right over . . . and uh, thanks for thinking of me."

Within five minutes he was there, cleaning up the jelly and broken glass from my kitchen floor. As I watched him wipe and sweep the linoleum, I was struck with awe at what my Lord had given me at that moment. Here was a friend going through a very difficult struggle of his own, but in all of his pain he was reaching out to help me. I saw in Scott, Jesus reaching out to me. Here I'd thought I would be the one to bring Christ to him.

I stood humbled, soaking in the love of our Lord, realizing for the first time on my own that Jesus cares about every detail of our lives—that he is a very personal God. I know that Jesus suffered and died for my sins, rose from the dead, and will come again to judge the living and the dead, and also to bring us who are saved by his blood home to heaven.

But to think He cares so much about a broken jar of jelly and the damage this could have done to my hands, after what he experienced on the cross, was a lot to take in. There in my kitchen, I closed my eyes and thanked God for this lesson.

Over the months, it became apparent that Scott was searching for answers in his own life. It was a privilege to be used as an instrument by God, because soon after, I was able to share with Scott what Christ had done for him, for us all. Many months later, Scott and his wife reconciled their marriage and worked hard to protect their family life.

I was beginning to see that the Lord had bigger plans for me than I could imagine. Pressing into the plan He had for me was frightening at first, but I soon understood that I could relax and he would direct my path. I needed only to follow and listen to His still small voice speaking gently and lovingly, leading me on this journey. Through following Christ, I came to understand joy, and that all things work together for His purpose.

The many long hours that had been invested in me during my childhood and early adulthood to someday enable me to live independently from my parents were paying off. Although I had never expected to move across the country, this proved to be the challenge I needed so I could understand how capable I was of living on my own.

In California, I learned about my abilities on the job and about my physical limitations, including knowing when to get help on my own, as well as my desperate need to put my trust in God.

I experienced the very normal emotions that come with change and uncertainty. What made this experience different was not giving up. I continued moving forward. I had a desire to be independent of my parents, which is God's plan for each of us, and so I was not going to let cerebral palsy handicap my life.

2

Exchanging Sunny Skies for Snowy Slopes

*"Don't let what you cannot do interfere
with what you can do."*

COACH JOHN WOODEN

After completion of R&D training in California, I moved back to Michigan with a new found confidence needed to live completely on my own. I soon bought a nice three-bedroom ranch on Rainbow Street, in Troy. I was no longer living just a few blocks from my parents, but I felt secure and excited about owning my own home, because now I didn't have to rely on my parents to get the help I needed in times of trouble.

My career progressed at IBM, and within six months I had received an excellent review, the best ever in all my time there. This review proved significant for my career, for within two weeks I was chosen to be enrolled in IBM's training program in Dallas, Texas. Training took eighteen months, and six weeks at a time were spent in Dallas learning to test and validate software developed for General Motors. At this time, GM was IBM's biggest customer.

After spending six weeks in Dallas, I returned to the Detroit office for several weeks and prepared technical reviews and configured systems. This rotation lasted the eighteen-month training period.

One interesting factor in going to an IBM training program is its competitive nature. IBM offers employment only to those college students who are in the top five percent of their classes. When sent to training, an IBM employee competes with the best of the top five percent of graduates from the most reputable colleges across the country.

Another extremely valuable part of IBM training was learning how to work with future customers. IBM puts a very high priority on this portion of training because a good relationship with the customer is considered the main ingredient of success.

Three weeks into my customer training, it was time to have a review of my presentation skills. IBM set up a management training team to role-play parts and gave us very demanding situations and problems we had to solve while maintaining a good working relationship with the customer.

Unfortunately, I had sensed from day one that the man who was to role-play my boss was uneasy with my disability. Sure enough, he gave me low scores, saying he felt my speech was an issue for the customer. My speech should not have been an issue; I had discussed it with other management people and knew that anyone who spent a few minutes with me could understand me without difficulty. It became apparent that my low score was a reflection of this man's discomfort with my disability and not my level of performance.

I couldn't accept the score I'd been given, and this became a major issue between the training class participants and the role-playing manager. The more I objected to the score, the more talking there was amongst the managers, which could be heard by almost everyone in the program. Soon this problem had made its way all the way to the top IBM managers.

After careful consideration, the management training team agreed that the score given me was grossly inaccurate and did not reflect my presentation skills.

I could not believe what happened through all of this. First, I learned to stand up for myself and not allow individuals to judge me based on my disability. Second, standing up for myself gave me a feeling of freedom. Third, in doing this, I forged a road in IBM for people who are challenged with disabilities.

For the first time, I began to feel as though God might be using me in this broken body to fulfill a deeper purpose than mere self-sufficiency.

I had the compelling sense that I needed to depend on the Lord, that this was his desire for me, and I wanted to please him. In addition, making it through this challenge ultimately made me feel very secure in my career.

It became evident that the Lord had truly opened doors for me, and in turn He allowed me great opportunities to open IBM doors for other disabled individuals. How privileged I felt to be used by God in such a magnificent way.

✷

Two years passed after completing my career training for IBM in which I devoted myself to hard work and growth. I was enjoying being back in Michigan and living in my own house, and by this time I had settled into a routine of working, paying bills, and having a good time with friends.

I'd met a good bunch of friends from a college-age singles group, and it amazes me how God brought me to these people. On April 6, 1981, my friend Joe Kleer ran into me at First Presbyterian, our home church. I remember this meeting very well, because just one week earlier the nation held its breath waiting to hear if President Reagan would survive the assassination attempt.

At our meeting, Joe told me about an exciting class he had just finished at the Shrine of the Little Flower Catholic Church in Royal Oak, Michigan. It was a Life in the Spirit Seminar, taught by members of the Love of God Prayer Community.

A man by the name of Jim Wyss had made a few announcements at the end of the seminar. After the seminar was over, participants mingled for a while. Joe ended up talking with Jim for several minutes and inviting him to a prayer breakfast hosted by the men's ministry of First Presbyterian Church. Our group met every Thursday at 6:30 a.m. in the back room of Howard Johnson's Restaurant in Royal Oak. So it was that I met Jim Wyss over our prayer breakfast one Thursday morning.

When I mentioned to Jim that I was looking for a young adult singles group, he had just the information I needed. I was interested in a singles group because most everyone my age at First Presbyterian was either married or well on their way, and it was hard getting together with friends who were all married or engaged. I found less and less in common with this group simply because we were in different phases of life.

Jim Wyss told me about the Young Adults group that his son attended. Jim invited me to dinner at his house so I could meet his son Steve and some of the other guys who were in this group.

"I wouldn't want to impose," I said.

"Nonsense," Jim replied. "This is a regular thing in our house! I promise my wife won't mind."

There must have been six college-aged guys around the big table, inhaling a scrumptious meal that Joan had prepared, and Jim was right: his wife seemed to enjoy feeding all the hungry appetites. No one at the table seemed bothered by my disability, and I felt very welcomed and accepted by this new group of single friends I had found.

At first I wondered if this Presbyterian would fit in with Catholics because of our denominational differences, but they never tried to convert me and indeed welcomed my differences.

Friendships developed rapidly. We spent time together doing Bible studies, playing softball and golf, and engaging in various other activities.

In the winter of 1982, I found out that my friends loved to ski. A friend from IBM owned a chalet in Northern Michigan located near Nubs Knob Ski Resort and it was available for co-workers to rent. I wanted to take some time off because I had been working hard to complete a project, and I thought renting the chalet and taking my friends for a long weekend would make a nice getaway. Besides, I hadn't taken much vacation time since I'd moved back home from California.

It was a brisk winter in 1982 and snow was falling softly from the sky when we gathered in a booth at Denny's on Woodward Avenue to plan our getaway. We sat huddled in our orange and yellow vinyl padded booth discussing available weekends.

"Are you going to ski, Larry?" asked Steve in his usual inviting tone.

"Not me!" I replied, with notable difficulty in my speech. "When I was seven I tried down-hill skiing and it didn't work because my legs were much too weak."

Marguerite took a sip of her hot tea as she thought for a moment. "Larry, you are much stronger now than you were at seven." Pausing for a brief moment and pushing her thick locks of chin length brunette hair aside, she continued. "Larry, you don't seem to have trouble with other activities."

There was a gleam in Marguerite's Irish blue eyes that told me she was not going to let me take the easy way out. "Come on, Larry, you are twenty-eight and strong."

Harold, who sat next to Marguerite, just had to chime in. "Come on, Larry," he said in a robust voice. "We have seen you golf, bowl, play racquetball, and softball. We'll help you all the way. Come on, what do ya say?" As Harold waited for a reply from me, his face broke out into a wide grin.

I looked at my three friends sitting with me in the booth, and feeling a twinkle in my blue eyes, I laughingly said, "You three have been after me for two weeks. What if I fall down?"

"We'll pick you up!" said Steve, who sat next to me in the booth. I was just kidding around, but Steve met my joke with serious and intent eyes.

I felt myself trying to squirm out of this situation. "What if you can't get me up?" I asked with slight panic in my voice.

In Harold's chiding way he tossed out, "Larry, there are three of us!" I began to feel that these friends of mine were not going let me weasel out of this experience.

As Steve finished his burger he wiped his mouth with a napkin. Smoothing his blonde hair to the side, he offered a suggestion. "Why not cross-country ski; you've done that before."

Harold remarked enthusiastically, "Now that may work!" His eyes widened, accentuating his wide grin.

"Good idea; you won't need to deal with speed or steering down a hill," Marguerite added.

Harold began to spell out the details involved in cross-country skiing on trails, while scratching his sandy blonde curls now and then.

Steve and Marguerite filled in the gaps of information as my reluctance gradually turned to a yes.

"So, skiing it is for all of us . . . Nubs

Knob . . . one cross-country and lift tickets for the rest," Marguerite confirmed as she dug into her salad.

Strong support flowed mutually between my friends and me. We'd all met through our young adult group, and we'd learned to encourage, challenge, and support one another in almost everything. Because we were such close friends, we also knew how to get on each other's nerves. This was one of those challenging, getting-on-my-nerves moments.

"Okay, but if I don't like it, I have you three to blame!" As I steadied my right hand with my left to manage a forkful of BBQ beef to my mouth, I had to laugh out loud at the way my friends had just talked me into skiing. It was a strange feeling as the four of us sat in that booth over a late dinner making plans for our trip. I felt twinges of excitement well up and my spirit began to feel light as I started to imagine being on skis again.

✳

A few weeks later, a crisp wind rustled through the pine trees, building anticipation and enhancing the mood for our adventure.

"Hold on, Larry, I just need to finish this lace on your shoe, then you can slip into your skis."

"Thanks Steve!"

"Slip the shoe in right here . . . hold onto my shoulder . . . okay, I think we got it," Steve said, with certainty in his voice.

When I stood up in the strange shoes, slipping them one at a time into the skis, I remembered the awkwardness of getting all the gear adjusted and feeling just right.

Marguerite handed me my poles. I managed the straps over my gloved, disfigured hands and began to maneuver with awkward difficulty, turning my steps into small hesitant strides.

Harold, Steve, and Marguerite stayed with me on the trails until I felt enough confidence in my skills to be on my own. Our foursome agreed to split up at this time. Off to the slopes the experienced skiers headed and I felt comfortable trying my endeavor solo, so I headed in the opposite direction toward the wooded trails.

"We'll take turns coming back to check on you, Larry," Marguerite shouted as she pushed her way through the snow toward the chairlift.

I managed fine after my friends left, and within a few minutes I was gliding under the snow-covered fir trees, which created a white tunnel all around me. My attention was so caught up in the beauty of the snow- covered trees that I didn't see the conditions ahead.

"Oh no! My ski . . . I can't get it up!" The tip had gotten caught under the snow. The snow had a crust-like layer on the surface, making it difficult to stay on top once it was broken.

With a tug upward, I tried to free my ski, causing me to slide backward, lose my balance, and fall down.

"I have to find a way up," I thought. "I've been alone for five minutes and look at this predicament."

Talking to the snow didn't help the situation, so I began to study the surroundings, looking for a way to get back up.

A voice called to me from behind, "Hey, you need a hand?" An experienced cross-country skier approached me.

"Sure do!" I responded, happy to see the young man and working hard to enunciate my speech.

The tall young man with dark curly hair finding its way out from beneath his knit cap offered a strong hand and support, pulling me into an upright stance.

"I was on my way back to the lodge and I saw you stuck here."

As I looked up, putting my trust in a stranger, we managed to secure my position back on my feet.

"Is this your first time on cross-country skis?" he asked.

"No, but it's been awhile," I answered.

"These aren't the best conditions under the trees," the man confirmed.

As far as I could see it was trees, and the path continued right under the trees, branching out in several different directions. It seemed that I was obligated in a forward direction if I wanted to continue skiing.

"I can't go back without giving it a fair try," I thought. "Thanks a lot for the help," I said out loud.

"It's okay, man. You all right?"

"Yeah, I'm fine now. Thanks again!"

The young man turned and headed back in the direction of the lodge.

Once more I tried to glide forward under the snow-covered trees. The tunnel offered little opportunity for fresh snowfall and the warmer temperatures from the day before had caused a slight melting of the snow, creating a crusty layer on the surface of the path. The sun was shining above the trees as the clouds moved off into the distance.

The wind picked up, blowing a gust that tousled my blonde hair around the edges of my blue ski hat. As I pulled my scarf up around my neck, I set off to try again. Over and over, I struggled to get up after falling down, then I would glide a few yards only to meet the ground again.

All morning it was the same thing. Getting up, skis catching in the crusty snow, another rescuer.

"I give up!" I thought. "This is not my idea of fun." Daily, the basic routines of walking, talking, dressing, and eating were monumental tasks. Being out cross country skis was supposed to be a good form of exercise and pleasure, not an experience filled with exasperation and torture. I fell again.

In frustration I removed the skis from my shoes and determined that was my last fall. I worked hard to pull myself up using one of the skis and then I strained to walk in the direction of the lodge.

"What am I doing out here?" I thought. Feeling angry and frustrated, I poured my thoughts and emotions out to God as I walked.

"I can't do this . . . This is crazy . . . Who am I kidding? This body is so limited! Did you make junk, Lord? Well, it sure seems that way to me!" By this time I was shouting out loud.

Feeling angry, overwhelmed, and ready to go home, I sat in the lodge, wondering what my response would be when my friends emerged, telling their wonderful tales of gliding gracefully down the slopes.

"Larry," came a concerned voice entering the lodge. "We were looking for you on the trails."

I looked straight up at Marguerite and began pouring out my miserable ordeal as we sat in the fire lit room. "I never should have gotten onto skis again . . . " My voice trailed off with frustration and disappointment.

By this time Steve and Harold had found us, completing the group and making it a foursome again. There was a sense of defeat in my tone as my friends sat with me by the fire, taking in every detail.

They listened intently to my misfortune, and the recurrent theme was how hard I had tried. "I was looking forward to exercising and having fun," I commented. "I just couldn't keep my skis on top of the snow."

My arms strained in awkward movements to describe the details of falling. "I kept falling . . . it's too exhausting to keep getting up off the ground." I went on and on, describing my attempt on the trails.

Harold, Marguerite, Steve, and I stayed in the lodge together for an hour or so, discussing the problem out on the trail. As I spoke, it became apparent to me that the crusty snow was the real problem, and I did realize that my first rescuer had warned me about the conditions.

"If only the conditions were better, I think I would have done okay," I said disappointedly.

"Too bad," Harold said, feeling somewhat responsible for the mishap. He continued, "The snow was great on the slopes, fresh powder. If you'd had those conditions you would have had no problem."

Just then, Harold's eyes widened and his face turned bright with an idea. "What if we ask at the counter if you can just try a run downhill to see if you can do it?"

Much to the surprise of my friends, I blurted out, "I'm game for that; I don't want to waste our time wondering if I really could have skied!"

With determination we took turns explaining the details at the ticket counter.

We were met with a staff that was not only intrigued and amused but also eager to help. "Here," the young man said who was behind the counter, "a free tow and lift ticket for the rest of the weekend."

The other young man and a young woman behind the counter stood watching with curiosity while the first young man tagged my coat zipper.

The young woman asked, "What is your shoe size?"

"Eight and ten-and a-half," came my unusual answer.

"Two different sizes?" she asked, more curious than ever.

"Yup, my right is an eight, and left is a ten-and-a-half."

After rummaging around behind the counter for a few moments, she handed me the mismatched pair of boots and skis, then remarked how she had never witnessed anyone so determined. "Good luck, and I hope you have fun," she added as we moved toward the door.

After all the problems I'd faced on the trails, things were beginning to look up.

My friends must have looked like a pit team at a Nascar Race, huddled around me. "Snap the boot; slip it into your binding . . . hold onto my shoulder . . . other side . . . snap . . . slip . . . clip."

The team worked with me, explaining what the straps on the skis were for, how to slip into the bindings, what to do if they should come off, how to shift body weight, and the many other details I needed to take in as a new downhill skier.

When it came time to try the bunny hill, they showed me how to gently grasp the towrope and gradually tighten my grip to catch a ride to the top of the beginner hill. Not having fine motor skills made gripping the towrope difficult. I wasn't going to let this stop me now. I grasped the rope and I felt a strong tug and jerking motion pulling up the side of the hill. When I reached the top, I released my grip very naturally and planted myself at the top of the small inclined hill. Steve moved out in front of me.

With confidence in his voice, he said, "Bend your knees . . . put the tips of your skis together."

Steve bent down next to me, holding my ski tips together, explaining to me how to snowplow moving down the hill.

"Hold your poles to the sides and use them for balance," he explained.

I tried my best to use the poles, but they kept getting in the way. "I can't seem to get the hang of using the poles," I said. Every time I tried to balance with them I fell because of the uncontrollable movements in my arms. The poles would catch the snow at strange angles and cause me to wipe out.

"Maybe if I just hold onto your shoulders I can get the feel," I suggested to Steve. This was somewhat awkward, but it seemed to work a little better going down the hill.

Back at the top I put the poles down. Again we tried to snowplow down the hill, and this time Steve was backward, facing me, holding the tips of my skis together, and I was holding onto his shoulders.

"Here we go!" shouted Steve. "That was a great run, Larry!" he announced with success in his voice as we reached the bottom of the hill.

With my friends taking turns helping, I practiced the snowplow down the hill over and over again. This scenario stirred much attention. It was quite a sight! I was surprised at how quickly my balance developed as I gained more skill with each run and learned from each fall.

Finally, Harold picked up the poles and handed them to me, saying, "Time to go it alone, buddy."

I took the poles in my hands, looked intently at them for a moment, and said, "These feel too awkward. I want to try without them!" Without delay, I handed the poles back to Harold and moved toward the towrope.

Grabbing ahold gently, then gradually tightening my grip, I felt confidence rise inside me. I knew deep within me that I was going down that hill, and I felt a freedom I had never known before. This was a desire I wanted to pursue. I could see my friends waiting, watching at the bottom of the hill with great anticipation.

"There he goes," Marguerite whispered. As she held her breath in nervous excitement, she prayed, "Lord, help him stay up on his skis."

A gentle rock forward sent me gliding down the hill in an almost sitting position with my skis in nearly perfect formation. My arms jerked about to maintain balance. Feeling the cold breeze nipping at my face, I couldn't help feeling a rush of excitement rise inside, which turned into a prayer of thanksgiving. I made it to the bottom of the hill on my own!

This was amazing! I felt as though God had given me a gift. Through this gift I was able to experience for a brief moment a release from the hold cerebral palsy had on me. What freedom this was for me! "Lord, thank you for this victory."

"He's actually doing it without poles!" Harold said in amazement.

Steve was speechless, his mouth open as if to say something, but all he could do was keep his eyes fixed on me.

Everyone who came out to enjoy the slopes that day had to take notice of what happened on the bunny hill. As I came sliding down to the bottom of the hill, loud, spontaneous celebration broke out. It was as though I had won a gold medal.

With tears in her eyes, Marguerite encouraged me. "You did it! You truly are an inspiration!"

With that cue, Harold, Steve, and Marguerite all took turns hugging and congratulating me. They'd known there was a depth of determination in me, but to see it put to the test was a miracle!

By the end of the weekend I was an enthusiastic downhill skier, graduating from the bunny hill and towrope to the chairlift and intermediate hill. I was amazed that I learned to ski without using ski poles! After we left the slopes to go to dinner our last night, I told my friends what I'd felt as I'd experienced freedom beyond belief.

I told them how hard it is to be stuck in a body that will not do what I need it to do. What freedom I'd felt, soaring like an eagle across an open sky.

I related being stuck in this body to being stuck in a fallen world of sin. When we receive Christ and turn from sin, we can have incredible freedom as well.

The sense of anticipation I had starting out on this adventure helped me understand that it is God the Father who calls us. It is through Christ that we are able to answer His call to be his child. And, I realized that I can do all things through Christ who gives me strength!

Some may call me crazy for taking such a risk as downhill skiing with my disability, but I think it mirrors what God wants to do in our lives. He does not want to leave us handicapped in sin but to give us new life to glorify him.

Walking in God's love and forgiveness brings tremendous freedom, similar to the freedom I experienced the first time I soared down the slope. If I'd had it my way, I would not have let my friends talk me into such a stunt and I would have missed out on incredible pleasure and adventure.

Thankfully, God had another idea for my life. When I sensed that something was stirring in my soul, I did not realize that it was something bigger than me. I am humbled, knowing that God can and will use me in this body.

After this ski weekend in the winter of 1982 came to a close, the long ride home was filled with the anticipation of an annual ski event. Sure enough, every January for the next six years, a weekend of renting the chalet and skiing at Nubs Knob was the destination and highlight for a few of my friends and me.

In between annual trips, I tried to ski locally as much as possible to get in all the practice and pleasure I could.

———

3

You Are Standing on Holy Ground

✳

"Before I formed you in the womb I knew you, before
you were born I set you apart; I appointed you as a
prophet to the nations."

JEREMIAH 1: 5

"I will praise you for I am fearfully and wonderfully
made; your works are wonderful, I know that full well."

PSALM 139:14

In 1981, my brother Steve married a wonderful woman, Stephanie. It was through the course of wedding preparations that I met Jeff, who soon turned out to be a really great friend.

We frequently got together to play a game of racquetball.

Our friendship grew over the next couple of years, and we enjoyed challenging each other on the court. Since we were both single, we had time to spend on activities such as golf and basketball as well.

Jeff worked for Campus Crusade for Christ at Indiana University. He kept the same schedule as the university and came home to Warren, Michigan, over breaks, which gave us time to meet on the racquetball court.

Jeff had been with Campus Crusade for a few years and I was already settled into my career at IBM, but I still made time to hang out with Jeff when he was home on breaks.

In 1983, the Saturday following Thanksgiving, Jeff was home on break and we got together for a friendly game of racquetball. Back when I was in college, I'd developed a great serve on the court and was pleased that I could score points with it.

Since beginning work full time after college graduation, practice time on the court was less frequent, but I was still counting on my serve for this game.

Jeff, on the other hand, must have been practicing while working on campus, because his return left me feeling as though I was playing in slow motion. He had me running all over the court, while he dominated the game. Wow, I was feeling rusty! I guess I'd been spending too much time in the office.

While we played, Jeff talked about a conference in Kansas City where Josh McDowell would be speaking to 25,000 college students.

Jeff seemed to really anticipate this upcoming event and all the excitement surrounding it. The more he talked about the conference, the more I wished I could go, but with work obligations, I didn't see how I could squeeze a conference in. Nonetheless, the more Jeff spoke, the more evident it was that he was hinting I should go along.

When I sensed his backhanded invitation, I served my response as though it were a racquetball.

"I really wish I could go, but I can't take time off of work. There are so many responsibilities getting my projects in on time."

"That should get Jeff to stop talking and hinting," I said to myself. I thought it would be fun to go, but I convinced myself my workload would not allow me the flexibility.

Just as I did not expect Jeff's return of my serve on the court, he delivered a sly and cunning response, simple but packed with power: "You keep saying you wish you could go; well then, come on!"

I don't know if Jeff realized what effect his words had that day, but they did cause me to pray about this conference after we finished our game and parted ways.

I told the Lord in the car as I drove home that I needed a sign. I felt like Gideon laying out a fleece. I knew this decision could never equal what Gideon had to do fighting the Mideonites, but his actions recorded in the pages of the Old Testament helped me understand that I could ask God for wisdom and direction in any situation.

I soon arrived at my Troy home, and parking my blue Chevy Blazer in the driveway, I noticed the mail had come early. The mailbox was next to the front door, attached to the brick, and the lid was propped open from the overflowing mail. It was a good reminder to take it inside.

While sorting through all the junk, a large folded piece of paper fell onto the floor from the kitchen table. Normally this would have waited to be picked up and tossed after I was finished sorting, but as it fell, I noticed something peculiar. The poster had Josh McDowell's name on it, advertising the very conference Jeff wouldn't stop talking about!

It was so obvious that God had a plan for me to be there that to think I was going to use work as an excuse not to go was unimaginable! Since I hadn't really spent much time vacationing with the exception of my annual ski trip, this conference provided a great opportunity to spend some banked vacation time. I made plans to spend the Christmas holiday with my relatives in Indiana before boarding a bus to Kansas City.

Jeff ended up leaving for Kansas City one day earlier and he put me in touch with his roommate, Doug, an interesting fellow who had a lot going for him. He was a dynamic Christian, and was the head coach for the Indiana University Women's Volleyball team.

Soon after we met, we boarded the bus to Kansas City. The conference was to start the next day, so Doug and I rode all night to our awaited destination.

It wasn't long before we struck up a conversation about where God was leading us in our lives.

I shared with Doug that I was feeling unsettled, perhaps disrupted in my spirit lately. Up to this point in my life I had been used to accomplishing four-year goals. I would soon be going into my fourth full-time year at IBM, and I was beginning to wonder if getting up, going to work, and collecting a paycheck was all there was to life.

Doug listened carefully, and though he didn't really offer advice, he spoke about where God might want to take us next. At some point during our conversation, he pulled out a brochure for the Holy Land. He said that Josh McDowell would be hosting the tour. I still had no idea who Josh McDowell was, except that he was speaking at this conference I was heading to.

I politely thanked Doug and slipped the brochure into my briefcase, which I'd happened to bring so that I could get some work done in the evenings. After putting the brochure into my briefcase, it fell into the abyss of the forgotten. My briefcase had become the "catch all" for loose paper, undone projects, and important articles. Needless to say, I soon forgot about the Holy Land brochure.

When we arrived at the Kansas City Conference Center, I was stunned by the number of students climbing out of busses, who'd traveled here just as I had. Jeff had told me 25,000 college students were coming, but to see them all at once was amazing. My mind was trying to take in so many students in one place who trusted Jesus as their Lord and Savior.

Doug and I walked to Adams Mark, where we were to meet Jeff. Once we were all together, the three of us checked in for the conference. Sessions began at 1:00 p.m., so we returned to

Adams Mark, our hotel, and took the opportunity to catch a nap to be ready for the busy afternoon and evening ahead of us.

Kansas City was an exciting town to be in. Our hotel was across the street from Arrowhead Stadium, home of the Kansas City Chiefs football team. Next to Arrowhead Stadium stood the Kansas City Ballpark, home of the Kansas City Royals baseball team.

Down the street from the stadiums stood the Kansas City Convention Center, where we met for the conference. Everything was within walking distance and very convenient.

Josh McDowell spoke at the New Year's Eve evening session, and something inside of me needed to know more of what he was speaking about.

He talked about how Christians spend so much time wondering what it is we are supposed to be doing. Though Josh spoke to the whole crowd of 25,000, his words specifically challenged me.

"If you are wondering where you are going, pray, and step out in faith. Don't worry! God will open and close the doors. If you trust the Holy Spirit to guide you, he will not let you go through the door he has closed," Josh said.

How often we think we need writing on the wall before moving in any direction at all. Josh's words penetrated my being. There had to be more to life than church, work, and paychecks. I now had a desire awakened in me to explore my walk with Christ in a new way.

I felt a strange prodding, perhaps better described as a journey, waiting for me. All I knew was it had to be where I needed to go. I was being asked by the Holy Spirit to trust.

What would happen next? How did Josh McDowell know to step out in faith? How did he know not to worry? He spoke so clearly and directly to me! I was very impressed with his ability to communicate.

As an IBM employee, I was trained to get out in front of customers, so I could appreciate what Josh did that night. How could he know all the answers my soul was searching for? I had to know what made him tick.

I spent December 27, 1983, through January 1, 1984, at this conference, learning that I could put my questions into words describing my longing, and that I could take the journey I felt waiting deep within my spirit.

By January 4, 1984, I was back at work in the Detroit office, and I soon learned that I needed to take a business trip to Dallas at the end of the month. Since I was traveling to Dallas, I thought it would be a good idea to stop in at Josh McDowell's Ministry Headquarters, also in Dallas. I called ahead from Detroit and spoke to Bob, who was Josh's ministry director.

Bob agreed to meet with me. I sensed he was having a hard time understanding me on the phone due to my difficulty in articulating my speech, so he made our conversation very short.

I was not sure at the time, but Bob did feel uncomfortable dealing with my disability over the phone. Later, he confessed that he held a preconceived idea that if I sounded so poorly over the phone, I must not be very bright.

Nonetheless, Bob agreed to meet me after he understood that I had a computer science background. We made arrangements to meet at 4:00 p.m. the afternoon I flew into Dallas.

After getting through the airport, then renting a car, I spent three hours on the Lyndon B. Johnson freeway stuck in traffic. I finally arrived at the ministry headquarters at 4:15, only to find that Bob had left for the day.

I was stunned! I could not believe I had missed him by fifteen minutes, and I couldn't help thinking some pretty nasty things like, "What kind of a ministry is this? They knew I was coming and couldn't wait just a few more minutes? How selfish!"

Nonetheless, I decided to stop back before going home to Detroit. This time I made sure I was there early in the morning to wait for Bob. As we talked, Bob inquired about my career with computers. To my surprise, he offered me a job doing all of the ministry's computer work.

All I wanted was to meet Josh McDowell to understand why his speaking was so intriguing, not take a job offer. After Bob pitched a job offer, getting me out the door seemed to be his goal.

After a brief prayer and an exchange of well wishes, thinking we would never see each other again, I once more left that office feeling like I had run into a brick wall, though I was still strangely curious about Josh and his ability to speak so well.

I assumed it was not in God's plan for me to meet Josh McDowell, so I put the whole notion out of my mind, and I'm sure Bob put me out of his mind as well.

About seven months later, in late July, I had to bring documents to a custromer and present an IBM solution to their company's computer needs. I couldn't fit the documents into my briefcase, let alone close it, so I resorted to the torturous task of cleaning it out.

When I finally reached the bottom of the briefcase, I noticed something strangely familiar. "Josh McDowell's Evidence Tour." It was the brochure to the Holy Land that Doug had given me on our way to Kansas City last December.

I had forgotten all about it, but now I felt a sense of being drawn to go. If this were Josh's tour, maybe this was how I would finally get a chance to meet him and find out why his speaking was so compelling.

Without further thought, I began filling out the form and writing my check. After I sealed the envelope, panic rose up inside of me. "I have never been out of the country before, nor have I ever taken a vacation by myself!"

"I have never stepped out this far," I thought. Looking back, I can see how my move to California helped me take this step.

I flew out the evening of November 6 from Detroit Metro Airport. While waiting at the airport, I saw a couple with the same carry-on bag that I had, provided by the tour company. Immediately I introduced myself to them and we talked about what we hoped to see and experience in the Holy Land.

From Detroit, we flew into JFK International Airport in New York. Our flight out of Detroit landed at a gate furthest from the International gates at JFK. Of course, this meant a hike through JFK with my luggage. The nice couple I met in Detroit Metro gave me a hand with my bags, and we made it to the gate with a few minutes to spare. If I'd had to do this task alone, I probably would have missed my flight out of the country, so I was grateful to my new friends!

While approaching the gate of our departure, I recognized a familiar face—Bob's. 150 people were going on this trip and meeting at JFK, and the first face I saw was Bob's. Amazing! As quickly as my twisted legs would carry me, I made my way over to him to say hello.

Bob had a look on his face that told me he couldn't remember who I was. As he took a quick glance at the nametag I was wearing to identify me as an Evidence Tour participant, he said, "Hello, Larry!" We shook hands, and I'm sure he was wondering where he'd met me before.

After a few moments, he genuinely seemed to recognize me and was very uncomfortable around my disability. This was the very factor that had kept me from meeting Josh McDowell in the Dallas office. Now I had eleven days to tour with Josh and I was determined to speak with him.

The tour group boarded the plane and we flew to Amsterdam, then to Amman, Jordan. In the course of our flight to Amsterdam, the pilot announced Ronald Reagan's re-election. Most of the passengers broke out into spontaneous applause.

Our plane landed at 4:00 p.m. and from Amman we began our tour via bus by 5:15 p.m. The bus headed to the Allenby Bridge, which spans the border between Jordan and Israel.

Along the way we passed through a very mountainous region and then descended into the lush green Jordan Valley. The valley was full of rich agricultural land, primarily banana fields.

The question that permeated my mind was how the people Moses brought to the Promised Land had passed through this very rugged country. I could not imagine what it must have been like moving a nation of people on foot through this type of terrain. Freedom from their pain and suffering as slaves in Egypt must have been the motivation for the Israelites to endure this trek into the land of milk and honey.

The next day, November 8, we stopped at Mount Nebo, which is the highest peak of the Abarim Mountain Range. This is where the incident took place involving Balaam and the "talking ass" (Numbers 22:21-31) and where God buried Moses' body in a ravine.

Josh chose this sight to share from the scriptures and as a place for the group to worship. He talked about not having a "wait attitude." "Paul didn't have a wait attitude. Look what he set out to do when God got hold of him. He set forth bringing the gospel to many lands. He didn't sit back and wait for writing on the walls. He went over the edge. Step out this evening; trust!" Josh said.

He spoke with such conviction and truth, sharing scriptures and talking about people in the Bible such as the apostle Paul who waited for the Lord by stepping out. I likened Josh's example to a restaurant waiter who serves. He is busy waiting tables. The waiter does not wait for the customer to yell the order from his table in the dining room while he enjoys a break in the back room. Rather, the waiter proceeds to the table without being asked, and this is where he finds his task. Our focus can be on listening while we wait.

After speaking about Paul, Josh turned to the experiences of Moses. "You see, Moses used excuses when God called him. Perhaps Moses stuttered, and could not speak to his people. Or maybe he thought because of how he was raised by the Pharaoh's daughter, the Israelites would not believe him. Whatever the problem, Moses did not step out and trust God at first. Finally, Moses trusted after the Lord was firm with him. God had a job that he wanted Moses to do. How it must grieve the Lord when we do not respond to his calling."

"Hmmm," my thoughts responded, "If Moses had the patience to wander for forty years while waiting to hear from the Lord, than I can be patient enough to listen for a few days or months while stepping out in faith."

God used Josh in a very powerful way to motivate change and growth in me. My thoughts drifted this time in a different direction. "My life situation has always been finding a way to accommodate my disability." I was feeling angry that God had allowed me to suffer from cerebral palsy. My mind was suddenly brought back to where we were when Josh began to share a personal story about being healed of stuttering.

Then it hit me! God was asking me to trust him because he wanted to use me in ministry! I sensed the Lord saying to me, "I want to give you a voice, Larry."

"For what, Lord?" I asked. Then I understood. "Oh, that is why You brought me here, to give me a voice." The whole message that night was to step out and trust. "I do trust you, Lord!"

That evening after the worship service, I found Josh and told him what had quickened inside of me. I shared with Josh what I thought I heard the Lord saying to me. I also told him I didn't really want to be in ministry because public speaking was not my forte, nor did I want it to be.

I had learned to become successful in my safe world of technology, because too often I came up short on the measuring stick of judgment when dealing with people and their first impressions of my disability. "Why would God ask me to minister to the very ones who reject me?" I wondered. I sensed a real connection with Moses as he was standing before the burning bush.

"Josh, will you pray with me?" I asked. Josh and a few others prayed for me that night. Stepping out in faith, I felt the Lord telling me to go out and be a fisher of men.

For the rest of the trip, I was filled with nervous anticipation, wondering what else God might do in me.

Several days passed, and we saw so many historic, biblical places. Through these places and events, our existence today has been shaped.

It was fun to exercise my imagination when I saw the ruins of the Walls of Jericho, rode through Joppa on a bus, and wondered what Jonah must have felt like running from the Lord.

I swam in the Mediterranean Sea and I saw Paul's prison cell. I saw Temptation Mountain, where Satan tempted Jesus after his baptism. It was during visits to sights like these, discussing the events that happened in the pages of the Bible, that friendships were made and experiences were forged that lasted a lifetime.

On Sunday, November 11, the sixth day into our trip, we boarded a tour boat from the town of Tiberias on the south side of the Sea of Galilee. We were headed to the north shore to Capernaum. This area is where Jesus called his disciples and where he performed the majority of his miracles. It was a calm day on the water, which made it difficult to understand what the disciples experienced when Jesus calmed the storm and waves.

When our vessel approached the shore, the very house was pointed out where the paralytic's friends dismantled the roof to lower their companion down to be healed by Jesus.

Our guide was telling about the different miracles Jesus performed in this place. The sun was warm and shining down on the water and there was an incredible sense of peace and wonderment as I tried to imagine Jesus walking these shores and healing those in need. The closer to shore we came, the more I sensed that God wanted to speak to me again. I waited, listened. "Lord," I asked. "Are you going to heal me and give me a voice? This makes sense. Now I can tell everyone what You have done for me this day in Israel!"

As I got off the boat at the home of Jesus, I realized how many miracles He had performed there. I felt the Lord telling me to take some time to thank Him for the miracle of surviving my birth, and the miracle that was currently taking place in my life.

We soon arrived at a small town called Tabgha, about two miles southwest of the city of Capernaum, where Jesus fed the 5,000. There were ruins of structures that commemorated Jesus appearing after his resurrection. There were newer churches built around the existing ruins. This is where we held our worship service.

On the way to our chapel service in this town, I felt God's presence envelop me. In His presence I felt the Lord say, "Larry, I really love you the way you are."

During Josh's talk, I was convinced I needed to ask forgiveness of someone in the group. Then Josh pointed out the need to forgive ourselves after asking forgiveness of someone else.

After the Sunday morning service, Josh and I sat at the foot of the cross in the church. We prayed together for the healing I sensed in Capernaum. Josh asked a special prayer that he be reminded each day for the rest of the trip to pray for God's will in the area of my healing.

What came to mind as we prayed was a question.

"Am I more effective today the way I am, or being totally healed?" At this time a scripture was revealed to me. Jesus told Peter he would build his church upon the rock. All I knew about this reference in the Bible was that Jesus claimed to be the rock of salvation. It occurred to me that it does not matter what our physical conditions are. God can use us. We don't have to be perfect, or the best looking. God will take us and use us just the way we are. He is God, and only he can make such things happen.

On Monday, November 12, 1984, Josh McDowell baptized me in the River Jordan. This was a huge step because here at this historic riverbank was the very first time I'd ever made a public confession of my faith in Jesus Christ. I had always believed in God, but now I was trusting my God. I desperately needed to give the Lord my trust.

This was the perfect time to be baptized. Through the experience of baptism and the confession that Christ is Lord of my life, I gained a confidence in Christ. What happened next, I don't know quite how to explain, but I was strengthened. It was not my strength, but the strength of my Lord and Savior who rose from the dead.

The last evening we spent in Jerusalem, Josh gave a talk called "Who Am I." "Each person is made in the image of God," Josh began. "Each person is unique. If I act like someone else, who will act like me?"

Again the words that flowed from Josh were speaking to me. Josh continued, "God is bigger than our weaknesses. He will use our weaknesses as our strong points in our Christian witness."

Hearing these words made me think of the scripture passage 2 Corinthians 12:8-10: "Three times I pleaded with the Lord to take it away from me. But he said to me, 'My grace is sufficient for you, for my power is made perfect in weakness.' Therefore I will boast all the more gladly about my weaknesses, so that Christ's power may rest on me. That is why, for Christ's sake, I delight in weaknesses, in insults, in hardships, in persecutions, in difficulties. For when I am weak, then I am strong."

After Josh finished speaking, it hit me between the eyes that my physical disability is my weakness, but the Lord is and will be using it to His glory. This was the reason I journeyed down such a path in my life.

Going to the edge of expectation and being brought back was the only way I could understand what the Lord wanted to do with this life. He gently led me and never forced my compliance, but once I understood his heart for me, I could trust him with all that I am. He proved trustworthy, even though I in my small mind could not understand. He unfolded his plan for me one day at a time.

This is really a gift. If God were to show us the end result of where He is taking us, I think we would get in the way by taking our own route there. He knew and planned my racquetball game with Jeff. He planned for Doug to give me the Holy Land brochure. He planned that I should miss Josh McDowell in his office because the Lord wanted me right here *in* the Holy Land when I was ready to hear.

The tour came to an end, but there are things I will never forget that we all experienced along the way. Most of all, I will always remember to tell others what God is doing in my life. I knew God was calling me to speak about his grace being sufficient for me, and I came home a changed man.

Walt, Gerry, Harold, and Steve picked me up from the airport and gave me a nice welcome home. The five of us frequently hung out together, but tonight I just wanted to go home and reflect on my trip. In addition, I was feeling the jet lag. The four guys were headed to Windsor, Ontario, for an evening out, but I just wasn't interested.

They brought me home and I settled in. I sat in my recliner and began to think about taking the next step. I was so tired from eleven days of traveling and all my life-changing experiences that the next thing I knew, it was 7:00 a.m. I woke up in my chair, just in time to get ready for work.

HURDLING HANDICAPS

Speaking Ministries

4

Hurdling over My Handicap and into Ministry

✳

"One of the secrets of life is to make stepping stones out of stumbling blocks."

JACK PENN

"To keep me from becoming conceited because of these surpassingly great revelations, there was given me a thorn in my flesh, a messenger of Satan, to torment me. Three times I pleaded with the Lord to take it away from me. But he said to me, 'My grace is sufficient for you, for my power is made perfect in weakness.' Therefore I will boast all the more gladly about my weaknesses, so that Christ's power may rest on me. That is why, for Christ's sake, I delight in weaknesses, in insults, in hardships, in persecutions, in difficulties. For when I am weak, then I am strong."

2 CORINTHIANS 12:7-10

There we were, all of my Young Adult friends in my living room on a cold Friday evening in December. I enjoyed being a homeowner for the very reason that I had a place for my companions to gather.

It was so cold that no one wanted to go out, but rather enjoy a few hours together in my warm, cozy house. I enjoyed making everyone feel welcome and comfortable.

I remember one humorous situation in October of 1984. I had invited everyone over to watch the Tigers during the World Championship.

Shortly after the invitation, a friend from work called and said he had an extra ticket to the game that I could have. The ticket just happened to be in the front row, along the first base line, very close to home plate. How could I turn down such an incredible offer when the Detroit Tigers were winning their way closer and closer to the World Series?

I knew I had a bunch of people coming to my house, which caused me to wrestle over what to do. Should I cancel the evening for my friends?

Instead of canceling, my solution was to let them all in the door before turning to leave. As I was on my way out, they all inquired, "Where are you going?"

I answered them sheepishly. "To the game."

There were loud moans and looks of disbelief. "How do you get all the perks, Larry?" someone shouted.

So there they were, the whole gang in my house, ordering pizza and watching the Tigers win and trying to catch a glimpse of me sitting near home plate on TV. I told them I would wave.

Many good memories and relationships resulted from opening my home to my friends, and some in this circle eventually married.

On this particular evening in early December, we didn't feel like playing cards or watching a movie. A thought came to me. "You guys want to see my pictures of the Holy Land?" They had all seen my photo album, but I felt the pictures didn't do justice to the experience. That was when I had slides made.

Out came my slide projector loaded with pictures; it was the fancy carousal kind, popular in the eighties. Gerry, one of my friends, took a painting off the white wall and instantly we had a screen for viewing.

As I clicked to each picture, telling about my experiences, the room would fill with roaring laughter or reverent silence. I never expected to see my friends wiping tears from their eyes when I told how I thought God would heal this twisted body.

The reaction when I finished presenting my slides was one of encouragement to tell my story. What I did not speak a word about to anyone was how I, like Gideon, had laid out a fleece to the Lord in the Holy Land, or how I'd prayed with Josh McDowell before my long trip back home.

I had asked the Lord, "If giving me a voice to tell of your goodness is what you want to do, then Lord, show me. Give me ten places this year to share my story, speaking to audiences outside of the church about who you are. What you want to do with me is more important than being healed."

There in my living room, after my slide presentation, I was being encouraged to do just what I had secretly prayed for with Josh.

In January of 1985, Hurdling Handicaps Speaking Ministry was born. By July of this year, I'd had ten opportunities to speak and six months of the year were still left! By December of 1985, the Lord had provided nineteen different opportunities for me to tell my story.

By the time the tenth speaking opportunity came, I felt very secure in my presentation. I would open with this infamous quote: "You claim you're no preacher, but preach a powerful sermon each day. The acts of your life are the things that you teach and not just the things that you say."

This quote reminded me of Moses, a powerful man used by God to free the Jewish people who were enslaved to the Egyptians. Moses had an excuse for everything. He stood before the burning bush, where the God, I Am, revealed himself, making excuses as to why he was not the man for the job.

I could relate to this! I asked all the same questions of God that Moses did.

Moses tried to convince God that he was not a leader, just a pampered prince. Then he tried to tell God he didn't know what to say to the Israelites. After God told Moses he would give him the words, Moses tried yet another excuse: no one will believe a pampered prince! Perhaps he tried to tell God that his speech was not eloquent enough. Finally, Moses told the Lord he just was not interested and to send someone else.

God assured Moses he would be with him all the way. "I will give you the power needed to speak. My promise is with you. I will provide for your every need."

God does not want our assets, or our strengths. He delights in using our weaknesses so he can be strong. He will even use the most unseemly characteristic about us, whether it is physical, spiritual, or emotional.

I always tell my audiences this: "We all have handicaps. The only difference is, you can see mine."

We look at the outward appearance when it is beautiful and assume God will use it, or we turn our attention to dwell only on our strengths, thinking this is what God is interested in.

I love the following word picture that explains this: take a candle and put it under a clay pot. Not much light will emerge from the pot, and perhaps the flame will go out. However, if the pot has cracks or even holes in it and is placed over the lighted candle, the light will shine through what we think is just a broken piece of pottery. Truly, our brokenness is what God desires. He desires to use us so that we may shine his light into the darkness.

Romans 12:1-2 says, "Therefore, I urge you, brothers, in view of God's mercy, to offer your bodies as a living sacrifice, holy and pleasing to God—this is your spiritual act of worship. Do not conform any longer to the pattern of this world, but be transformed by the renewing of your mind. Then you will be able to test and approve what God's will is—his good, pleasing and perfect will."

It occurred to me as I stood on Mt. Nebo in the country of Jordan, learning about the exchange between Moses and God, that I was about to enter the Promised Land. This was the spot where Moses first saw the Promised Land. Moses did not get to enter into the land of milk and honey. Moses died upon this very mountain, and God buried Moses there.

I realized I did not have to miss the opportunity God had for me. If I were willing to step out in faith, God would be faithful in giving me a voice to speak. He would give me provisions and power, and his promise would be with me every step of the way. What I received as I began to do public speaking was the same promises God had given to Moses thousands of years before.

These promises have been kept. In 1985, Hurdling Handicaps Speaking Ministry began and established its first ministry board. Ten years later the ministry hired its first employee.

Lori Thomas proved to be a huge blessing. Before she took the position, I was working full time at IBM, speaking part-time, and doing all of the administrative work for the ministry. The ministry board proved to be a great asset, keeping the direction of the ministry accountable to God's vision and purpose.

In the last twenty years, the Lord has opened doors for me to speak that I never dreamed possible. He sent me, in this twisted body, to inspire and bring hope to so many who needed encouragement.

I have been sent by the Lord to minister to professional sports teams such as the Detroit Tigers, the Detroit Lions, and the Boston Red Sox. I've spoken at youth rallies across the country, at prayer breakfasts, and to youth groups. Churches have booked dates to have me speak at their services. The Fellowship of Christian Athletes makes sure I come back every year. I minister to Youth for Christ, Campus Crusade, and to youth camps both Christian and non-Christian across the nation.

I have opportunities to address kids of all ages, from preschool through college. My largest audience was about two thousand people and my smallest was just a handful.

As I began my speaking ministry, I saw the lives of people change. Many reached out in faith to discover what God had planned for them to do. In my own life, I try to always step out, because I do not want to regret not knowing what God intended for me.

Many stories have inspired me, some well known by the public and some not so well known. I remember when Dave Dravecky, a famous baseball player, lost his arm and shoulder to cancer, and when Joni Eareckson Tada became a quadriplegic after a diving accident severely injured her spinal cord.

For these two individuals, life seemed hopeless. Perhaps it was, but God took their brokenness and used it so His voice would be heard.

I think of Eric Little, the famous Olympic runner. He was a missionary to China who knew God had a purpose for him to run in the games.

In one part of his story, his sister was not pleased that he was going to participate in the games. She put much pressure on him not to run. His response to his sister was amazing: "I will go back to China, and be a missionary, after I run. My heart is in my mission work, but I also know that God made me fast. You see, when I run, I feel God's pleasure."

I could see what God had done for me. He molded this life in a twisted body to be used for his glory. God did not want to use me way off in the future, but right now. What does God want to do with you?

When we answer God's calling in our lives, we are fulfilled. Sometimes tragedies occur, but remember this: what Satan intends for evil, God will use for good. That is why He is God. He will gently remind us through His mercy that his promises never fail.

Jeremiah 29:11 says, "'For I know the plans I have for you,' declares the Lord, 'plans to prosper you and not to harm you, plans to give you hope and a future.'"

The Master potter fashions the vessels for his use. We can trust him, because he will lead us into the promised land.

5

One One-Hundred-Dollar Bill

✳

"It's a recession when your neighbor loses his job; it's a depression when you lose yours."

Harry S. Truman

"Turn to me and be gracious to me, for I am lonely and afflicted."

Psalm 25:16

"I waited patiently for the Lord; he turned to me and heard my cry. He lifted me out of the slimy pit, out of the mud and mire; he set my feet on a rock and gave me a firm place to stand. He put a new song in my mouth, a hymn of praise to our God. Many will see and fear and put their trust in the Lord."

Psalm 40:1-3

I stood before a group of college-aged single adults sharing an analogy using money. I reached into my pocket and pulled out a crisp, clean one-hundred-dollar bill. As I announced what I had in my hand, I held it high over my head for the crowd to see.

As I looked around the auditorium at the five hundred-plus single adults there, I asked, "Who would like to have this one-hundred-dollar bill?"

The auditorium was filled with excited murmurs. Of course, everyone in the auditorium raised his or her hand.

Then I said, "Just a minute . . . " I took the crisp one-hundred-dollar bill and began to crinkle it in my twisted hands. After I had sufficiently wrinkled the bill into a ball, I dropped it on the ground and began to step and stomp on it.

I then picked the tattered bill up and tried to smooth it out while everyone was watching. I held the bill up again and asked, "Is this still worth a hundred dollars?"

There was silence for a moment while the crowd thought about my question, and then a resounding "Yes!" rang out when they realized it was still money. Then I began to explain the significance of this demonstration.

"You see, everyone is valuable to God, no matter what shape we are in. The Lord loves us unconditionally. Sometimes we see ourselves only through the eyes of sin. Perhaps we have an addiction, or are emotionally unstable. Maybe we're stuck in guilt or have an incurable disease.

"Though the world may see you as crumpled, you are still valuable to God. God wants to heal our unseen handicaps and meet our need to be loved. He may not heal us physically, but he will heal our broken spirits. If you begin to see yourself the way God sees you, you will begin to see a different you."

I went on to explain how, in the Gospel of Matthew (9:20-22), a good example is given of how we can reach out to receive what God has for us: "Just then a woman who had been subject to bleeding for twelve years came up behind him [Jesus] and touched the edge of his cloak. She said to herself, 'If I only touch his cloak, I will be healed.'"

The woman in this culture was unclean. This meant she could not mingle with the rest of the population because of her condition.

How often I have felt this pain of rejection because of my disability! My body is twisted, my speech is unclear, and I cannot control the movements of my body. When I go out in public, people stare and children ask their parents what is wrong with me. I used to let this emotional pain tell me who and what I was: unclean! I could relate to this woman in scripture.

As a teen I became very self-conscious about my appearance. I began to doubt my worth as an individual. I would sit home on Friday nights while my younger brother Steve went out on dates. No one wanted to go out with Larry Patton. I was lucky if I could get a date, let alone a second date with the same girl. I remember asking a friend in high school to go to my senior prom. She was like a sister to me so I know it was safe to ask her.

As I grew older, into my twenties, I desired to be married and have a family. Again, dating was difficult. Women would tell me they would go out with me only as a friend. There were many lonely nights and feelings of inadequacy. "I'm not worth as much as everyone else," I felt. It was easy to use this sentiment as a crutch when I was turned down for a date. I was empty and longing for a soul mate, especially when my friends began to get married.

One by one, my male friends each found the woman of their dreams. I lost several roommates this way. The joke was, if you want to find a wife, just move in with Larry and you're sure to find your woman within six months.

I went to wedding after wedding after wedding, all the while feeling miserable inside. I put on a good front on the outside, because I truly was happy for the couples getting married, but it was tearing me apart on the inside. I wanted to be up at the altar taking their place instead of watching as their guest.

This area of my life was very difficult to give over to God because I thought he did not have a wife for me. It was also very frustrating continually battling my sexual desires, and I had trouble believing a woman could ever be attracted to me. I saw myself in the mirror every day. I couldn't blame a woman for not wanting to take on a husband with my disability, and I was angry at God.

I identified with the Israelites wandering in the desert after leaving Egypt. They wandered in circles for forty years! My heart was hungry like they were hungry. I needed water to quench my thirsty spirit, and a warm shelter for my soul.

Angrily, I asked the Lord, "Did you take me to the barren desert to forget about me?"

God responded to my lonely, angry heart. He understood rejection. "Men rejected my son," He told me. "Jesus went to the cross to provide an invitation to the wedding feast I will have in Heaven, and he is still rejected to this day. Jesus was lonely when he asked his disciples to keep watch with him in the garden of Gethsemane. How my son wept over Jerusalem and longed to gather them under his wing like a mother hen gathers her chicks."

Gradually, as the Lord spoke to my heart, I heard him say, "Only two things I ask of you. Love me and serve me." That is all God calls us to do. When we love him and serve him, Our Lord will provide what we need.

So many times in my life I have taken my eyes off Jesus and begun to walk on my own. I could not trust Christ with my singleness because I did not want to accept being single for the rest of my life. I was weary of carrying this angry burden of my singleness.

After going to a friend's wedding I found myself desperately crying out to God, begging him to please take my singleness and make me content with it. For the first time, I understood that God wanted to be my first love. God knows it is best for us when we put him before anything or anyone else. Loving the Lord with all of our being is what brings contentment into our lives, but sometimes it is very difficult to give up the desires we so desperately want. When Jacob wrestled with the Lord, Jacob did not give up until his hip was touched and broken by the Lord. I too wrestled with the Lord. I needed to allow God to break my will so he could heal my heart. Finally, for the first time, I came to understand that God does not love married people more than single people. I then had to ask myself if physical image is everything. After all, our society is consumed with looking at the outward image.

Even in our wilderness, we can reach out to the Lord for the healing that our hearts desperately need. We can love God today in our deserts, In 1 John 4.19, we are reminded, "We love because he first loved us." He knows the unseen handicap keeping us lost and wandering in the desert. I always knew that God loved me because he sent Jesus to die for me, but I was never sure if God *liked* Larry Patton. This was a huge handicap in my life. The handicap in me was not the body I had, but my inability to love myself.

When I began to see myself as Christ saw me, I knew I was likable. I didn't have to impress anyone anymore. I did not need to find my worth in the judgments of other people. I wanted the Lord as my first love, and I knew he could build on this foundation if he chose to.

It was still difficult at times to see my married friends, but holding tightly onto the cloak of Christ encouraged me.

A story I like to share when I talk about unseen handicaps involves a man who stopped at a garage sale. He looked around and found nothing he was interested in. As he turned to leave he caught a glimpse of something under a tarp sitting in the garage. What he soon discovered was a Harley Davidson motorcycle.

The man asked the owner if he was interested in selling the bike. The owner said, "Sure. Give me fifty dollars and I'll help you haul it out of here. It's missing a few parts and doesn't run anymore."

The man quickly paid the fifty dollars and with the help of the owner loaded the bike into his truck. "I never owned a motorcycle before," he thought. "I wonder if I can fix it up?"

When the man came home he examined the bike and found where the missing piece should go. He immediately found the number to the local Harley Davidson dealer. He told the dealer the year of the bike and proceeded to order the parts.

A few days later, a phone call came from the dealer. He told the man he needed a serial number off the bike and that he would walk the man through the process of finding it.

The man took his cell phone to the garage and began following the instructions given to him over the phone. When he took the seat off the bike, the dealer asked him what it said. The man answered, "The King."

When the dealer heard this, he said, "Sir, I have been authorized by Harley Davidson to offer you $300,000.00 for this bike." You see, it had been Elvis Presley's motorcycle.

We may not know what we are worth, but God does. I was once like that "worthless" motorcycle hidden under a tarp. Perhaps that is what you are feeling today. But when the *King of Kings* inscribes his name upon our hearts, we become a priceless treasure.

6

A Lifetime Investment

"By the grace God has given me, I laid a foundation as
an expert builder, and someone else is building on it.
But each one should be careful how he builds. For no
one can lay any foundation other than the one already
laid, which is Jesus Christ. If any man builds on this
foundation using gold, silver, costly stones, wood, hay or
straw, his work will be shown for what it is, because the
Day will bring it to light. It will be revealed with fire,
and the fire will test the quality of each man's work."

1 CORINTHIANS 3:10-13

"Hello, Larry," I heard the woman's distressed voice say on
the other end of the line. "My mother is hospitalized and recovering from a major heart attack. I wanted to let you know because it will be some time before she is able to get back to work."

The woman on the phone was Mrs. Campbell's daughter, and Mrs. Campbell had been my housekeeper for three years. She knew where I liked everything put away, she always folded my socks the way I needed them, and she even converted my shirts from button-up to Velcro. Not only did she make my house sparkle, she knew how I liked things done in my home.

Now I was faced with interviewing housekeepers and getting used to a new one. I'm sure there were many capable of doing the job, but I must admit, I am very particular.

In the beginning of her employment with me, Mrs. Campbell came right in and was no nonsense. She could anticipate my disability needs and she did a remarkable job caring for my home when I could not. Her lifetime investment was serving others, and in her grandmotherly way she made sure I had a conscience.

She would take a moment to leave a note telling me, "Jesus and germs are everywhere, so wash your hands and say your prayers." She would also tell of what God was doing in the life of her family every time I stopped home to pick up a forgotten item.

Come to think of it, she actually trained me in her way of doing things, and this is where I learned to be so particular. Mrs. Campbell and her abilities would be sorely missed in my home. I had to trust that the Lord would provide for my needs.

At the end of June, a friend called me to ask if I had a housekeeper yet. When I told her I did not, she responded with, "I could fill in for you until you find someone to replace Mrs. Campbell. I am off work for the summer and could use the extra cash."

Jenny had graduated from college in 1982 and now, four years later, was between jobs. She was a good, trustworthy friend I'd met through Young Adults. It seemed like a perfect solution to hire her. I told Jenny we could give it a try, but I warned her that I was used to Mrs. Campbell's style.

This did not seem to bother Jenny, so she started the job the following day. To tell the truth, I was relieved to have some help. I was having a hard time keeping things up on my own, and now I had a real appreciation for anyone who could do a good job cleaning.

I liked having my house clean because it was a meeting place on Friday evenings for the Young Adults group. We would get together, decide our Friday evening activity, such as a movie and dinner, or just hang out at my place.

Sometimes it could get pretty crowded with fifteen or more college-aged people in my living room, but Friday nights were always something to look forward to.

In June there was an annual Catholic conference held at the Notre Dame College campus. The Young Adult group, which was Catholic in origin, decided to travel to the conference together. I enjoyed fellowshipping with my Catholic friends and worshipping with them occasionally, but I didn't feel called to attend the conference.

Our usual Friday night came and everyone was at the conference. I thought I would be spending the evening alone when suddenly the doorbell rang. When I opened the door, I saw Jenny standing on my porch. She had come over to hang out.

"Come on in," I said. She glanced around and had a surprised look about her. "Is anyone else coming over?" Jenny asked.

"I think everyone is at the Notre Dame Conference," I answered. "We're the only ones left. I guess we could go see a movie." Jenny agreed, and we decided to see *Top Gun* starring Tom Cruise.

After the movie we headed to Pasqualli's, a fine Italian restaurant on Woodward Avenue. It was a normal evening, except the group was much smaller. We split a pizza and talked about the movie. The pepperoni must have clouded my thought process. I don't know why, but I was thinking about my background as a Presbyterian.

Suddenly I blurted out, "I don't know why I'm hanging around a Catholic Young Adult group. I'm not marrying a Catholic girl."

I'm glad Jenny was a good friend, because that was a really strange statement and she just took it in stride. That's what I liked about my circle of friends; we were good friends with no facades. I was glad for Jenny's friendship.

I remember the first time I met her. Jenny's existence was unknown to me until I went to her house in October of 1985 to pick up her younger sister for a date. Jenny became actively involved in Young Adults in late November of 1985, which impressed me very much; a young woman with an interest in her faith.

On Monday morning I had to make an unexpected sales call. I'd forgotten to grab my new business cards off my desk at home, so swinging by the house on the way to my appointment would allow me to pick them up and see how Jenny was doing with the housekeeping.

I entered through the front door and Jenny was wrestling with the hose of my very loud tank-type vacuum. When she saw me enter the house, a look of horror came over her face. I couldn't imagine what she was doing to create such panic.

Jenny fumbled for the off switch and the vacuum's noise slowly died down. "I didn't know you were coming home. You scared me to death!" she gasped.

"I'm really sorry," I replied. "I stop in from time to time to get things I leave behind."

Jenny began mumbling something about not being presentable. "I just threw on my old sweat clothes and I didn't really take the time to, to be, well, presentable. Larry, you caught me at my worst!"

I could hear her saying odd things about her appearance, but my mind was focused on getting my business cards. She was obviously feeling self-conscious about something.

"Oh," I responded, not really paying attention. Then it came to me that I could invite Jenny to the IBM picnic coming up in mid-July.

Every summer IBM held a wonderful picnic on Boblo Island. The company really supported family values and went out of their way to provide a memorable experience for parents and kids alike. Any employee who was single could bring a date. It really was an impressive event that anyone could thoroughly enjoy.

I thought it would be great to bring a friend from Young Adults. Since I was here, I might as well ask Jenny to go to the picnic next Saturday.

"Well, um, sure! I'd like to go," she responded.

The event was fantastic! The number of times we went on roller coasters was too many to count. We played games under the tent and indulged our appetites in the delicious smorgasbord provided for all employees and guests.

It was about 11:00 p.m. when we decided to leave. Most of the families with small children were gone by now, but we felt like kids having the time of our lives. I reached in the front pocket of my shorts for my car keys, and then began to pat all of my pockets.

"Jenny, did I by chance give you my keys?"

"No, Larry, you put them in your pocket," she said.

"My keys, they're gone!" I shouted. Panic rose in the two of us.

"How will we get home, Larry?"

"I have a spare car key at home," I offered sarcastically.

"A lot of help that is, Larry."

"Hey, hold on a second. If we could get to my house, I could get my key. Oh wait, that won't work, my house key is on my key ring that I lost."

"Larry! I have a spare key to your house. I use it to get in every time I clean your house."

"That's it! Now we just need to get to your house, Jenny." I looked for someone still there from IBM. I managed to find my friend Roy, and he gave us a ride to Jenny's house in Royal Oak.

We thanked him and he was on his way. Jenny walked up to the door and twisted the doorknob, but it was locked. She did not have a house key on her. Jenny rang the doorbell, but nobody was home. We'd made it this far, and we were stuck again!

Jenny's aunt lived down the street, so we walked there. No key to the house there, either. "I don't understand!" Jenny said.

"The door is never locked, and my parents are always home. Where would they be at midnight?"

She sounded as though she were the parent and her parents were the kids staying out too late. The only thing we could do was wait for Jenny's parents to get home. We sat on the porch yawning and talking about how fun Boblo Island was. Too bad the day was ruined when I lost my keys.

Headlights came streaming down the dark neighborhood street. Julianne, Jenny's sister, and Harold had just returned from their five-year high school reunion.

"Julianne, do you have a house key?" we both asked. "Where are Mom and Dad?" Jenny added.

"I don't know," her sister replied, "and I don't have a house key." Harold disappeared for a few minutes. Unbeknownst to us, he had spotted an open window on the second floor. He came running to the porch from the curb, yelling that he could get in.

"What are you talking about?" Jenny asked.

"Look, up there. I can get up there from the porch structure and climb through the open window," he said.

You have to understand Royal Oak homes. There are no two alike. To describe the house Jenny lived in is quite a task, but I will try. It was an older home, with three stories. The front porch was more like a stoop, with a storybook roofline about eighteen inches wide outlining the front door and rising up over the front living room window.

Harold stepped up onto the rail surrounding the cement porch and pulled himself up onto the storybook roofline. He carefully walked as far up as he could to the top above the door. He was standing on a point, which would be the top of an upside down "V." The open window was slightly to the right above the front door.

Harold worked to get the screen free from the window frame; he then tried to climb in legs first. Julianne, Jenny, and I stood just in front of the porch, watching and holding our breath.

"He did it!" I shouted. All I could think about was getting to my house to retrieve my spare car key. Just as Harold opened the front door, Jenny's parents pulled up in the driveway.

"What is Harold doing in our house?" they asked with curious expressions. After a lengthy explanation, we were on our way with my house key to my house in Troy.

It turned out to be a long night. After getting the car key, we had to drive all the way back to Detroit's dock parking for Boblo Island. Once there, I finally unlocked my car and followed Jenny all the way back to Royal Oak and then went home to Troy.

By the time Jenny was returned safely home, it was 2:30 a.m. I was thinking sarcastically to myself on the way back to my house, "Wow, I really know how to show someone a good time."

As far as I could tell, Jenny didn't hold the Boblo incident against me because she didn't avoid me at Young Adults on Wednesday nights. She was a great friend with a good sense of humor.

It was still mid-July, and a friend of mine, Dave Ray, whom I met on the Holy Land Tour, had a daughter who was getting married in mid-August. I sent the RSVP back with two attending. I did not really enjoy weddings. It echoed the lonely feeling that with this disability there could never be a wife for me. "Lord, I would like to go and enjoy myself. Help me find a date who will not make excuses or turn me down when I ask her to go."

Immediately I thought of Julianne Ebaugh because I had dated her before. I had about four weeks to find a date. After praying, I picked up the phone to dial Julianne's number. She answered the phone.

"Hi Julianne, this is Larry. Hey, I have a wedding to go to in August, and was wondering if you wanted to go with me?" After telling her the date of the wedding, she said she already had plans. She said she was sorry.

After I hung up with Julianne, I picked the phone back up and pushed redial. I figured I could ask her sister, my friend Jenny. After a few rings, Jenny picked up and answered.

"Hi Jenny, this is Larry," I said. "Um, I have a wedding in August and wondered if you would like to go with me?"

"Sure, I'd love to," Jenny replied.

"Wow," I wondered, "why didn't I think of asking her in the beginning? That was easy!"

Jenny and I made arrangements for her to meet me at my house before the wedding because I had a golf outing with the First Presbyterian golf league that day. She had a key, so she could let herself in and wait comfortably.

As bad luck would have it, my foursome ended up behind four of the slowest golfers on the planet. Meanwhile, Jenny was at my house, waiting and waiting for me to show up. There she was, all dressed up, waiting in my house for a guy she probably thought was a real "winner". . .

It was getting later and later on the golf course and I began thinking about all the times I had gotten together with Jenny and of all the crazy things that had happened. "First I think out loud in the restaurant, then I lose my keys at Boblo, and now I'm stuck on this golf course!"

I was feeling my agitation grow, knowing I was late with every minute that clicked by. "Three strikes and you're out," I mumbled out loud. "I am certainly not the most impressive guy to be with. She will never speak to me again!"

Needless to say, we missed the wedding ceremony. We did, however, make it to the reception. When we arrived at the hall in Birmingham, we snuck right into the receiving line without being noticed. All of the women guests were given a Christmas ornament hand decorated by the bride. This ornament roused my curiosity because I love Christmas and all the trimmings.

My house was the one all lit up at Christmas time on Rainbow Street. I have had a love for Christmas lights and decorations since I was a small boy.

Jenny was engaging with the other guests and I was politely thinking of a strategy to get her new ornament. I was thinking that it didn't make sense for her to have the ornament, because she didn't know the bride. I decided to behave and not covet Jenny's new ornament.

When we stepped onto the dance floor, I sensed God telling me that if I would just shut up and behave, the Christmas ornament would someday be mine. We dined, we danced, and enjoyed the evening together. I was glad I had asked Jenny to go with me. She seemed very natural to be around and I didn't have to be something else for Jenny to enjoy being with me.

The evening was winding down at about 12:30 a.m., so we decided to leave. We drove back to my house so Jenny could get her car to drive home. I parked in my drive and invited Jenny inside. She reluctantly said through a yawn, "Alright, for a few minutes."

A few minutes turned into hours while we discussed our hopes and dreams and shared the many personal issues we've had to endure. There we were, sitting together on the sofa talking, and I had never seen Jenny look so beautiful before.

The more we talked, the more I couldn't take my eyes off of her. I knew these emotions welling up inside. I was afraid of all these feelings because they had so often been met with rejection. Time and time again my disability had caused women to pull away.

My heart began to pound because Jenny was right beside me and I was falling in love with her. I knew I could no longer ignore what I felt awakening inside of me.

Jenny seemed to have a glow about her. She would look into my eyes when she listened to what I was saying, and when she spoke to me depth and emotion stirred my soul.

I leaned closer to her. She didn't move away. I was sure she could hear my heart beating out of my chest, and still she remained close. I was leaning so close that I could hear her quiet breaths. She turned to look at me and I kissed her gently. She didn't move away, but welcomed my kiss. She soon left for home and I was left breathless.

The next morning in church, I told my mom that I'd found the woman I wanted to marry.

"Larry," my mom answered, not really believing me, "how many times have I heard you say that?"

I was so giddy I could only laugh when she said that. I began to date Jenny very seriously. After a few weeks of dating, a trip to Dallas came up. Before I left, we decided to each write ten questions we wanted to ask each other about our relationship, and we agreed to give answers to our own questions as well.

I was in Dallas for one week. While in Dallas, I had dinner with a friend of my mom's. Norma happened to be a family therapist. Over dinner, she helped me to formulate questions to ask Jenny.

When I returned home, Jenny and I had dinner together at a quiet restaurant. She started with her first question. "Do you want a family?" We discussed our answers.

Then I asked her two questions. "How would you resolve a conflict over a disagreement?" and "What do you think fair fighting should look like?"

Jenny looked at me with the strangest expression, asking, "Where did you come up with these questions? I feel like I'm being psychoanalyzed."

Nonetheless, she answered my questions and I answered hers. It actually took us weeks to get through all of them.

The week after I returned home from Dallas, which happened to be the third week in August, Jenny moved out of her parent's home and into the W.O.G. House. The acronym stands for Women of God. It was a rental house that four Christian women rented together, and I thought it was great because it was on my way home from work.

Stopping in on my way home quickly became routine for us. It was now well into September, and Jenny was substitute teaching, which meant there were no papers to correct. Her evenings were free and we spent every moment we could together.

It didn't take us long to know that we were serious about our relationship, and this prompted the hypothetical question of what we would do if we were engaged to be married.

Across the street from Jenny's home was a nice little park. If we felt we needed privacy, we could go sit in the park and talk. Our discussions frequently turned to our traditions in faith. There were differences between Catholic doctrine and Presbyterian doctrine to be worked out between us.

Somehow we came to the conclusion that we would not become engaged until these issues were resolved. Jenny and I compiled a list of ten couples on both sides of these faith traditions to see how they handled the issue. We found that some couples worshipped separately and others went to both churches, but split the time of worship to two weeks at one church and two at the other church.

By the time we finished listening to all of these couples, we were no farther ahead in our problem than when we started. Indeed, it seemed we ministered to several of these couples just by asking our questions.

Finally, we spoke to my pastor. He suggested we go to each other's churches and really get to know the traditions we came from.

We did as my pastor suggested and it worked for us nicely. We worshipped at First Presbyterian Church in Royal Oak one week, then the next week we worshipped at Shrine of the Little Flower Catholic Church, also in Royal Oak. Soon after we found this temporary solution working, we talked further. We came to a new conclusion: we would not get married until we worked out our differences.

I remember taking Jenny to my family's cottage for a weekend near Fenton, Michigan. It was a great place to unwind and relax. There was a golf course so close that my dad, brother, uncle, and I could walk right up to the edge of our property and onto the first tee.

The lake was on the other side of the cottage, making the whole scene look postcard inspired. I thought it would be nice for my family to meet Jenny and for her to get to know the Pattons better.

We arrived later than we wanted, and to my surprise, my dad and the rest of the guys were headed to the golf course already. I walked Jenny to the door and introduced her to the extended family.

Right after a quick introduction, I headed to the golf course, trying to catch the guys. When I look back, I cringe because I left Jenny with a houseful of people she barely knew, but she said she had a marvelous time hunting for antiques in town with my mom and aunt, so I was off the hook.

I knew I wanted to marry Jenny, but I wasn't sure exactly how she felt about me. Perhaps it was my own insecurity fearing another rejection that kept me from trusting our love.

The next Saturday after coming home from the cottage, I asked Jenny over the phone if she would go with me to see a movie. She said she was meeting a friend for dinner. Acting out on my insecurity, I immediately began to ask who "he" was.

Jenny laughed at me and assured me it was an annual meeting with a friend she had grown up with. Jenny and Susan had lived on the same street, had gone to school together, and had graduated together. Susan had since married a farmer from Canada, and this was about the only time they saw each other.

I could not believe the jealousy I felt, thinking Jenny was meeting another man over dinner. I was relieved it was Susan she was meeting with.

Jenny and I had seen each other every day since the wedding in August, with the exception of business travel. By now, I was trying to convince Jenny to speak to her parents about our relationship, which they had no idea was happening.

"Larry, I just moved out a month ago, and the last thing I want is to go home and tell them what is between us, only to have them disapprove because of your disability." I had to trust her since she knew her parents better than I did.

November 1, 1986, I began to search for an engagement ring. Jennifer wanted to make things official on Christmas Eve. I decided I would secretly ask Jenny's father for her hand in marriage. It was Wednesday, November 5, 1986, when I called up Jim Ebaugh, Jenny's father, to invite him out for coffee at Denny's (the same place I had planned ski trips with my friends) to discuss his daughter.

We met at Denny's on Twelve Mile and Woodward Avenue early that evening. Jim did not make this meeting easy on me. He spent a good hour talking about everything under the sun and not giving me a chance to say a thing. Finally he asked, "Was there something concerning my daughter you wished to discuss?"

His eyes were sharp and glaring and his voice resonated the following challenge: "This is my daughter and you want her hand?"

I proceeded to ask for permission to marry his daughter, Jennifer Ebaugh.

"Well, Larry, I don't think this is a good idea. I don't know you well enough," he responded.

I sat back in my seat, trying to take in what I thought I'd heard him say.

When it registered, I thought to myself, "Well, sir, I am not going to marry you!" I knew better than to say my thoughts out loud. Jim and I talked some more about my life and how I planned to care for his daughter for the rest of her life.

After another hour, Jim finally said, "I want to speak to my daughter about you. Based on what she says, I will either give you my blessing or not give it."

I had a speaking engagement in Keystone, Colorado, over Thanksgiving and Jenny was scheduled to come along to this singles conference. Her parents devised a plan to get her to come for dinner followed by a talk in the living room.

On Monday, Elaine, Jenny's mother, called and said, "Jenny, this will be the first Thanksgiving without you here; would you like to come to dinner tonight?" This meant we would not be getting together.

I remember waiting on pins and needles for her to call me that night. I knew in advance what was going to happen; now I had to know what Jenny's parents thought of me, and what they had discussed together.

At 10:00 p.m. the phone rang. It was Jenny. "Larry, you know how you have been after me to talk to my parents about us? Well, turns out they brought me into the living room [which was only used for company or interrogations] for a 'talk' after dinner to ask me about my relationship with you! Can you believe it?" Jenny had no clue I had spoken with her father last Wednesday.

"What did you say to your folks?" I asked.

"I told them I was in love with you and hoped to marry you some day. They just wanted to make sure I was all right with our relationship. They didn't try to talk me out of anything."

When I heard that, I felt as though I could relax now without the pressure of trying to convince Jim and Elaine Ebaugh that I was worthy of their daughter. I felt confident that Jenny's parents would have scrutinized anyone who might have asked for the hand of their daughter. This was the permission I needed to begin the process of asking Jenny to share a life-long commitment with me. Things were changing now. I was no longer shouldering a burden of having to prove myself to anyone. I felt as light as a feather.

In the past, I had struggled tremendously with romantic rejection. Sure, I did fine making a way to live with my disability in this world, but this effort did not quench the loneliness deep in my soul. I desired a soul mate, a wife of my own. I desired to have the companionship of a woman in a lifelong relationship, sharing everyday living together. I wanted to wake up to the day with the woman I loved by my side. How I longed to share the experience of decorating our Christmas tree together. I wanted to know what it would be like to bump into each other in the kitchen while preparing dinner together. I longed for a wife to lavish my love upon, and now it was happening to me.

My mind was consumed with thoughts of love for Jenny. I wanted to give her my very best; I needed to give her all of who I was. When I desperately surrendered my singleness to the Lord, I believe this act made a way for me to experience a deeper love. When I surrendered, truth became clear to me as though a veil was lifted from my eyes: I am loved with an everlasting love despite all the odds my disability throws at me, and never in my wildest dreams did I think I would know love so deeply.

I am not speaking of Jenny's love for me, but of a deeper, far wider love, the foundation I needed to base my relationship with Jenny on. It was the Holy Spirit that enabled me to grasp "how wide and long and high and deep is the love of Christ, and to know this love that surpasses knowledge—that [I] may be filled to the measure of all the fullness of God" (Ephesians 3:18-19).

Shortly after Jenny told her parents about our relationship, I found the perfect engagement ring for her. It was a beautiful solitaire diamond in a gold setting. I knew it was the ring for her when I set eyes on it. It was lovely, just like Jenny.

We left Metro airport on the Sunday before Thanksgiving. I had arranged for a layover in our travels to visit a couple I considered to be surrogate parents. Dick and Jeni welcomed us into their Mobile, Alabama home, and little did Jenny know that she was there on display! Every time she left the room, I would pull Dick and Jeni aside and ask, "What do you think of her?"

Dick was a friend from First Presbyterian Church and had been my youth advisor when I attended youth meetings there during high school. We had many youth who were on fire for Jesus, and this made a huge impact on Dick, causing him to enter the ministry in the late 1970s.

From Mobile we flew directly into Colorado. From the plane's window the mountains looked so refreshing covered with white, fluffy powder. I was thrilled Jenny could come along. This was the first time she would hear me speak since beginning Hurdling Handicaps. The whole conference centered on the question, "Does God have you where He wants you?"

I was going to speak on Thanksgiving evening, just before Elizabeth Elliot, the keynote speaker. This was one Spirit-filled woman, and I found it very humbling to be her warm-up.

In Keystone, the snow gracefully adorned the mountain slopes like a white satin shawl strewn across a high-back chair. It was a beautiful shuttle ride from the airport to our accommodations, taking in all the natural beauty surrounding us.

We had so much fun the day we arrived. The conference did not start until Tuesday morning, so after settling into our rented condominiums, we decided to take in some adventure on the slopes. We still had a couple of hours left Monday afternoon, and the whole evening to enjoy. I was in heaven it seemed, being able to ski Monday evening at Keystone and to have my girlfriend with me. Jenny put her heart into skiing, but didn't share the same enthusiasm I had for the sport.

After the conference ended on Tuesday, I again hit the slopes, this time with my condo roommate. Jenny spent her time reading publications given at the conference sessions, going to dinner with her roommate, and clicking the shutter on her camera capturing the beautiful surroundings on film.

Again on Wednesday evening I went skiing, after having dinner with Jenny, while she enjoyed spending time meeting new people and taking pictures of the scenery.

The next day was Thanksgiving and we had only two evening sessions scheduled, Elizabeth Elliot's and mine. The daytime hours were free time, which meant I could get in more action on the slopes. "Jenny, would you mind if I ski until about 1:00 in the afternoon?" I asked. I didn't want to take advantage of her good nature. We'd discussed it Wednesday evening and she really didn't mind.

The first thing I did after waking up Thanksgiving Day was send a dozen red roses to her condo; then I hit the slopes. As I was leaving out the door to go skiing, my roommate Brice shouted, "Have a good day!"

"Oh," I responded to his well wishes, "it is going to be a great day!"

After getting in from my ski rendezvous, Brice was gone. I showered, changed, and called Jenny. "Hi, Jenny. I'm back from skiing. Do you want to come over here?" I asked, feeling nervously excited inside.

"Okay . . . Let me finish my lunch dishes and I will be right over."

After I hung up the phone, I played with the stereo until I found a station that played love songs. It was 2:30 p.m. when Jenny arrived. I created a cozy, romantic atmosphere in the living room. When she entered, she kissed my cheek and thanked me for the beautiful flowers. We settled in quickly and shared how the conference was impacting us.

After a moment or two, I turned to her to ask her a question. Just then the door bounded open and Brice came in with a bag full of books he just purchased in the lobby. When he said hello, I looked at Brice and motioned with my head to leave and do it fast! I think he got the hint, because he cooperated nicely.

Jenny had a look on her face that told me she could not believe what I had just done. If her facial expressions could speak words, Jenny's would have said, "You are so *rude!*"

After Brice finally left us alone, I stood up and walked across the living room to the balcony door wall. What a beautiful moment this was. Jenny noticed the view outside and grabbed her camera. We were standing side by side looking out into the perfect beauty of the snow-covered mountains. The fir trees below were exquisite with white texture stroked about their branches, perfectly designed by the master painter. Jenny had no clue what was about to happen. I turned toward this beautiful woman and spoke softly.

"Jenny, I have to ask you a question." The anticipation was growing inside of me. I could not wait another moment to ask her what my heart desired.

She glanced at me and said, "Oh Larry, I just have to get a picture of this view!"

I watched her fumble with the camera for what seemed to be an eternity. All the while I thought my heart would burst as I waited!

After she got her picture, she turned to me, asking, "You wanted to ask me a question?"

I pulled my hand out from behind my back. I uncurled my fist to reveal a diamond ring. It was then that I asked, "Jenny, will you marry me?"

She stood there just looking at the ring.

"Oh, she needs to think it over," I thought fearfully.

She managed to speak as her eyes filled with tears, saying, "Yes, Larry! I will marry you."

Later she said she couldn't respond because she was so surprised. Jenny was expecting a ring and my marriage proposal on Christmas Eve. The funny thing was, I went skiing all week with her diamond ring in the breast pocket of my ski jacket. I did not want to lose it, so I kept the ring close to my heart. Of course, we had to call home to share our good news with family and friends.

As we were getting ready to leave Colorado to go home, ten inches of snow fell rapidly, delaying all flights. We were supposed to be arriving in Detroit at 8:00 p.m. on Saturday. We finally landed at midnight and there sat my parents, Bill and Sue, leaning on each other, dozing in the uncomfortable plastic airport terminal chairs.

Scattered about them were hand-painted posters congratulating us, made with special love by our friends in Young Adults. All of our friends had left for home because it was uncertain what time our flight would land. Mom and Dad were gracious to stay and wait since we did not have a car in long-term parking.

Jenny and I still had denominational differences to reconcile, and our decision was this: since we were now engaged, we would not get married until these issues were resolved. We would keep right on rotating between churches.

I was thirty-one years old and Jenny was twenty-seven, so we would try to work things out as soon as possible. I used to think thirty was over the hill, but now I could see that life was just beginning. We figured if we called our churches to find out how long in advance we would have to plan a wedding, we could come to an agreement on doctrine before the wedding.

Jenny called both of our churches and both had almost every weekend booked for weddings over the next eighteen months. We did not want to wait that long because of our ages. When a June date in 1987 at the Shrine of the Little Flower Catholic Church became available, we booked it.

We felt very fortunate to get the twelfth of June. This particular date was on a Friday night, which was good, but we had only seven months to prepare for our wedding and our differences to reconcile. Jenny and I trusted that the Lord would help guide us into agreement.

Coming to a resolution over our doctrines seemed critical now, so we devised a new plan after asking for the Lord's help: if we could not resolve our doctrinal dilemma, then we would not have children until we could work something out. We kept alternating mass and service and waited for the Lord to give us direction.

Jenny and I were married on Friday, June 12, 1987. My minister friend Dick, from Alabama, was there to co-officiate the wedding with Father Prus, the Pastor of Shrine.

After our honeymoon, we settled into my house on Rainbow Street. It was wonderful sharing my house with my wife, until she began redecorating. I guess I had been a bachelor too long, because I did not like the changes she was making. I was having a hard time adjusting emotionally to what she wanted.

Jenny began one project after another. I did not have the patience to go through this much redecorating and besides, this was my house; I'd paid for it. To settle our differences, we sold the Rainbow house and moved to Royal Oak, where we could make a fresh start together.

Two and a half years later, I asked Jenny's father if he still had the same concerns about me marrying his daughter. My father-in-law reassured me that I was the perfect husband for his precious daughter.

At our wedding reception, I gave Jenny a gift to remind her of my true and unfailing patience. It was an enlarged framed copy of the photo she had taken just moments before I proposed to her.

Now, Jenny would tell you this: if you knew me, you would understand that patience is definitely not my strong point. If Jenny only knew the patience I had, not to remove that camera from her hands that so rudely interrupted the mood and the moment when I was about to propose, she would feel differently. Well, I guess I have a lifetime to convince her otherwise.

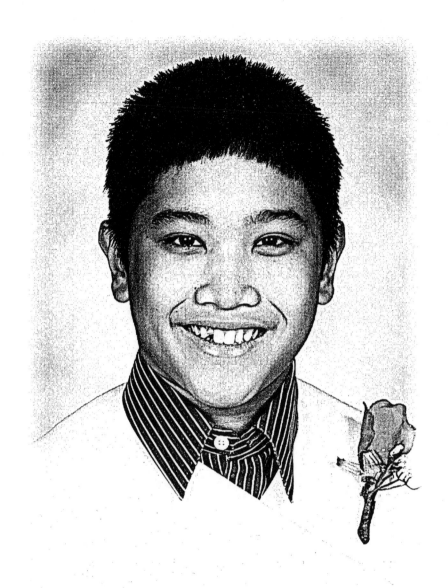

7

God's Good
and Perfect "Will"

✳

*"So if you faithfully obey the commands I am giving
you today—to love the Lord your God and to serve
him with all your heart and with all of your soul—
then I will send rain on your land in its season,
both Autumn and Spring rains, so that you may gather
in your grain, new wine and oil."*

DEUTERONOMY 11: 13-14

I could not believe the news I was hearing as we sat in our doctor's office. "We will need to do a few tests on both of you to find out why you're not getting pregnant."

Jenny and I sat motionless in the soft green chairs opposite the doctor's desk. After a few moments Jenny managed to ask questions regarding the procedures. I sat still, paralyzed in my chair, trying to digest this dizzying information.

Jenny and I had planned a big, beautiful wedding for June 12, 1987. We enjoyed the love and support we gave each other as a married couple, and I was especially glad to be by Jenny's side when she learned of her mother's illness just one short week after our wedding.

The formal diagnosis came in July of 1987, one month after our wedding. We were devastated to learn that Jenny's mom, Elaine, had ovarian cancer.

Being newly married, I tried to support Jenny in the best way I knew how. As Elaine went through surgery, followed by chemotherapy, I could see Jenny being swept away by grief over her mother's illness. I was devastated to see my new wife hurting so much and I felt completely helpless to comfort her.

I also knew how much Elaine meant to me and I could not imagine losing my mother-in-law. We needed her around to be grandma to the family we wanted to begin.

After our first year of marriage, we felt it was a good time to start our family. I had one brother and Jenny came from a family of six brothers and three sisters, so obviously family meant a great deal to us. Besides, it would be a bright spot in the wake of Mom's battle with cancer.

After our second year of marriage and another year of Mom battling cancer, we thought perhaps it was the stress of a sick mother that prevented us from conceiving a child.

We heard so many people say, "Just relax, it'll happen . . . don't worry, you'll see." But month after month, pregnancy test after pregnancy test, there was still no baby growing in Jenny's womb. The intensity to bear a child grew stronger every month.

"I want to have our baby," she would say, fighting back tears every time the news came of another friend's pregnancy.

I was desperate to help my wife! It hurt so bad to watch her grieve her mother's illness and endure the pain of being denied the one joy she so much desired. I wrestled with the fact that I could not give my wife the desire of her heart.

I knew I had to take our desire for children before the Lord. I was afraid to do so, because I felt it would be a crushing blow if God should answer us with a "No." I was not willing to take that risk and further my wife's despair over our infertility.

During this dark time, Elaine had another surgery, followed by another round of chemo, tightening the circle of stress by which we were bound. Adding to the pressure, most of our friends had two or more children by now and we couldn't help but notice.

Finally, Jenny and I decided we needed the help of an infertility specialist. As her husband, I was determined to find a solution to this problem. If this doctor said it was hopeless, I would find another.

After all, my life up to now had been one big story about overcoming obstacles. Why should this be any different? Hard work and determination had always conquered and won out in the past.

We decided to begin the tests our doctor recommended, followed by various procedures, and month after month a pregnancy test was our focus. Every time a new procedure was done, another pregnancy test followed. As always, it had the same result—negative! We began seeking professional help to deal with the devastating emotional aspects of our infertility.

During the third year of our marriage, Jenny's mom had one more surgery, followed by more chemo. It was becoming obvious that Elaine could not beat the cancer, and Jenny became focused on her mother during her last days. All told, Elaine had battled cancer and undergone three year's worth of surgeries and treatments.

My wife spent as much time as possible with her dying mother, and the two talked for hours, with Jenny listening to what at any time could be her mother's last words. Elaine knew how desperately Jenny wanted to have a baby, and she was saddened by her daughter's struggle.

"Jenny," she said, her name spoken so tenderly, "I hope and pray you have a baby soon . . . I would be so happy to see my daughter with the desire of her heart before I am home with the Lord."

How I wanted to give Jenny a baby, to soothe the ache of losing her mother. Neither Jenny nor I could understand why God would not give us a baby!

Babies were everywhere. At the school where Jenny worked as a teacher, staff members had babies on the way. In our Christian Married Group many women were expecting, and in Jenny's own family, several sisters and sisters-in-law had babies on the way. We counted fourteen babies due that year.

We felt surrounded and trapped by our infertility problem. The grieving and infertility became an intensified circle of pain, but only a few people knew about our troubles. When we went to church and saw friends, they would ask the standard, "How are you?"

Well, you don't respond by saying, "Terrible! Let me tell you about our infertility problems." That just isn't done!

Jenny's mom, Elaine Ebaugh, took her last breath on September 16, 1990. Sadness filled my wife and she could hardly stand up under the weight of her grief. As Jenny mourned the loss of her mother, the infertility issues continued to loom. Bigger waves of sadness came and pushed my wife under. It was as though she were drowning.

"Oh God," I would pray, "please send my wife, send us, something to hold on to!"

One week had passed since we'd buried Elaine when I received a phone call from my brother. Steve and I were very close and talked frequently on the phone before starting work in the morning. We had a good relationship and talked about everything. He knew the trauma we were experiencing and he was a good support to me. I was glad to have a brother who cared so much.

Steve and Stephanie had married six years before us and I had been best man in their wedding. Little did I know at the time of their wedding that in a few short years I would meet the woman of my dreams—Jenny.

"Larry," the voice came over the phone. "Can Stephanie and I come over tonight and talk to you and Jenny?"

"Steve, we can talk on the phone," I replied.

"I'd feel better if we could come over tonight."

"Okay, I'll let Jenny know." I couldn't imagine what was so important that they wanted to come over to say it.

It was about 7:30 p.m. when the doorbell rang. When I opened the side door of our red brick ranch home in Royal Oak, I felt the humidity of the unusually warm September evening drift in behind Steve and Stephanie.

"We just came from Mom and Dad Patton's and thought we should come over to tell you first, so you won't hear it from someone else." Steve sort of hung his head as he blurted out these words.

I couldn't imagine what he wanted to say. "Are you two okay?" I asked, wondering if perhaps their marriage might be in trouble. Steve and Stephanie seemed to have a great relationship, and being just the two of them, they could focus all their attention on their music ministry.

I glanced at Stephanie, who seemed to be struggling with something that needed to be said. She could not take her eyes off of Steve, and her look told him it was time.

"Larry, Jenny, we are going to have a baby. You're going to be an uncle." Steve and Stephanie grasped each other's hands and tears filled their eyes. Stephanie began to cry softly because she knew how difficult this news was for us to hear. Steve gently put his arm around his wife and the tears fell from his eyes.

By the grace of God, Jenny and I were able to muster enough courage to congratulate them. Somehow I managed to ask Steve, "How long did you try?"

"Four weeks," he responded.

I was in shock. I didn't know it was possible to conceive in just four weeks!

My brother and his wife did not stay long enough to sit down, and when they left, Jenny and I struggled to accept their news. Steve and Stephanie originally hadn't even wanted kids; how could it be so easy for them to conceive? I didn't understand. We had been trying to have a baby for years.

After the news sunk in, we were truly happy for them, but at the same time it was the straw that broke the camel's back. I remember them saying goodbye and hearing the door close behind them. As soon as the heavy wooden door latched shut, I saw my wife crumple to the living room floor and the sound of her crying was more than I could bear. I fell to the floor with her, my arms around her, and we cried for a very long time.

I knew then that we had to go before God with our infertility, and I finally faced the fact that I could not give my wife a baby. I could not fix my infertility problem for her, and she could not fix her infertility problem for me. We were confronted with the pain infertility caused in our hearts. We knew that God was using Steve and Stephanie's baby to drive us to our knees before him. How God longed to bring us into his good and perfect will.

✳

Four months passed after falling to the floor in our living room crying out to God and giving him our infertility. We desperately needed a vacation, so we packed our bags and headed to Florida and spent time on the beaches near Tampa.

It was a warm winter in Florida, so we spent most of our time talking over our life situation as we soaked up the sun, relaxing at the beach.

One day as we sat talking, digging our toes in the warm sand, the idea of adoption came to us. A spark of life leaped inside Jenny and I could see it in her eyes. The more we discussed the idea, the better it sounded. We had no clue how to go about adoption, but we knew we could ask Jenny's brother and sister-in-law, Paul and Marsha, and our good friends, Chuck and Joann. Both of these couples had adopted through reputable Christian agencies.

As soon as our vacation was over, we knew we had to pursue this avenue to have the family we so desperately desired. We prayed on the beach together that if it was God's will, he would set everything in motion, and if not that he would close the doors to adoption.

After spending a week in Florida it was time to head back up north to our home in the snow. When we walked in the house, we noticed a call on the answering machine from Jenny's dad.

"Hey Larry and Jenny, if you could call me back I have some details for you. Your cousin Becky called to ask if Paul and Marsha wanted to adopt another child. Seems she knows someone who is in a troubled situation and wants to put the baby up for adoption. I called Paul and Marsha and they were not interested, so I called Becky back and told her you guys might be interested. Hope you don't mind me taking the liberty. Anyway, call me back and I can give you the details."

Jenny and I must have stood in the kitchen for a good five minutes before either of us could speak. "How did they know?" Jenny asked. No one could have known what we discussed on the beach in Florida! We were awestruck at what was beginning to unfold. We knew we had to pursue this child. We laughed and cried, thanking God for showing us his tender mercies.

As we got set up with a reputable out-of-state Christian adoption agency to manage the details for us, we never anticipated the amount of paper work to be done and the many interviews with adoption personnel. Our caseworker said that my disability would need to be included in our records. We tried to convince our caseworker it did not need to be included, but we soon learned this could not be negotiated, period!

Once we understood this, Jenny and I immediately set to work filling out numerous papers, having people write up references for us, and getting our meetings and home evaluations scheduled. We finished all the requirements in two weeks.

Our caseworker could not believe the efficiency with which we worked. To tell the truth, Jenny and I had no idea how long the average process took. We were amazed when we were informed it could take three months or more. Again, we could see God's hand at work in our lives.

After all the papers were turned in and our file was complete, we became keenly aware that a person with a disability is usually not the preferred parental choice of the birth mother. This made us very anxious and again drove us to our knees, but this time a calm settled over us as Jenny and I prayed and asked our Lord for the strength to trust him.

We heard nothing from our agency for many months concerning the adoption of the baby we were told of. On an early May morning in 1990, sun poured into our kitchen window facing east as the phone rang.

"Hi, Larry, this is Steve. Stephanie just went into labor and I am taking her to the hospital." Jenny heard me answer the phone as she entered the kitchen to put her empty juice glass in the sink.

Our eyes met and I saw a strange peace in my wife. She whispered to me, "Tell them we will be praying!" I told Steve we would be praying before saying goodbye.

"Jenny, you look beautiful today!" I told my wife.

"Thanks, Larry," she replied as she smiled and kissed my cheek.

I left for work and Jenny and I waited anxiously all day to hear the news of our niece or nephew's birth. When I arrived home Jenny was there preparing dinner. "Any news yet?"

"Not yet. Could you set the table, Larry? Dinner is almost ready."

I opened the cupboard door and started to take the dishes from the shelf as the phone rang. We looked at each other and then raced to the phone. Jenny got to it before me.

"Hi Steve . . . a boy or a girl?" she blurted into the phone.

I saw Jenny's mouth drop open and I could not imagine what was going on from the other end of the line. As I was soon to learn, it was Cathy from the adoption agency.

"Your baby boy is waiting for you," Cathy said to Jenny. "If the two of you can come in first thing in the morning, we can go over all the details of getting your baby into your arms." Jenny looked so overwhelmed!

"Are Stephanie and the baby okay?" I asked. Jenny started laughing and crying as she told me what Cathy had said. Jenny said goodbye to Cathy and hung up the phone. I turned Jenny toward me and gently held her for several minutes.

I whispered to my wife, "Congratulations, Jenny! I mean Mommy!"

And she responded back, "And you too, Daddy!"

A few minutes later the phone rang again. This time it was Steve. "Hi Larry, we have a baby boy! His name is Jonathan!" Steve said with all the joy of a brand new father.

"Congratulations, Steve! That is great news, we are so happy for you two." Steve told us that Stephanie and Jonathan were doing great.

"Steve, we have great news also. We just got a call five minutes ago telling us that we have a baby boy waiting for us!"

Steve and I were so excited to know that we both had sons, boy cousins born only a few weeks apart!

Jenny was so happy. It was wonderful to see my wife smiling and laughing again. "Larry," she whispered, "I want to stay home with our son. I want to be there for our child." I felt confident in my wife's abilities, so we made plans for her to be a stay at home mom.

The emotional labor we had endured seemed to fade away as we held our baby boy in our arms. One of Jenny's sisters made known to us that it was exactly forty weeks from Elaine's death to receiving the call telling us our son had been born.

We traveled out of state to the adoption agency where our little baby boy was being readied. He was waiting for us in a baby seat placed on the table in the reception room.

As I looked at my new eight-week-old son, William James Patton, he held up his arms to me as if to say, "Daddy, Mommy, I love you!"

We spent the afternoon navigating a strange city to find the courthouse where everything would be made official before a judge. Our little William James who was named after both of his grandfathers seemed to enjoy being toted about the city.

The judge who handled our case had questions about my disability. "Can you care for this child? Can you work and provide a living for this child? Are you sure you can do what is needed for this child?"

"Yes, sir," I answered, "I work for IBM and have passed all of our home studies, which are included in our file."

"Isn't IBM a computer company?" the judge asked.

"Yes, sir, it is."

"Well, Mr. Patton, I am confident that you have a secure living. We won't keep your family waiting any longer." With that there was a stamp of approval on our adoption.

Our baby boy was wide-awake in his car seat as we made the long trek back home, and he has been wide-awake ever since.

"What do you want to call him?" Jenny asked.

"My dad goes by Bill; it would be nice to call him something a little different. How does Will sound?"

"I like it!" Jenny said. It was quiet in the car for a few moments as we rode along the highway.

"Oh, Larry," Jenny whispered as she wiped tears from her eyes, "it is hard to take in what has just happened for us. God truly gave his good and perfect 'Will' to us!"

8

High-Tech Security Blanket Has a Short Circuit

"He has no hands but our hands
To do his work today,
He has no feet but our feet
To lead men in his way;
He has no voice but our voice
To tell men how he died,
He has no help but our help
To lead them to his side."

WILLIAM BARCLAY

The applause was thunderous as I walked up to the podium to receive the First Annual Disabled Computer Scientist of the Year Award in March of 1993 for starting a new program at IBM helping disabled employees and customers tailor equipment to their special needs.

I remember it was a cold Thursday evening for Washington D.C. The awards evening was hosted at the Washington Hilton Hotel, and Senator Bob Dole presented the award. This was the highlight of my career, and I took the day off from work to travel to D.C. for this unforgettable event.

I had been with IBM for seventeen years at the time I received this honorable award, and IBM was a superb company to work for. Not only did it treat its employees with the highest regard, it was known to go out of its way to take care of them. I was fortunate to have landed there when I did. All throughout my college career, IBM invested in my training. The beauty of getting into IBM when I did gave me seniority over many who were just graduating from college, which meant a very stable job. In fact, I made plans to retire from IBM when I turned fifty-three with full benefits.

The new program I'd begun at IBM was inspired in the summer of 1990 when a customer who was losing his sight came to me for help. Max felt comfortable telling me about his problem reading the monitor of his computer. He knew I was transparent about my disability and he respected my honesty concerning it.

As we discussed his needs, the idea came to me to modify his computer system, resulting in consistently larger print, which would make it easier for Max to read.

In July of 1990, President George Herbert Walker Bush signed into law the Americans with Disabilities Act. This meant that businesses had to make the workplace accessible to all people by adding entrance ramps, accessible restrooms, and equipment that would help the disabled better do their jobs.

This law opened up a whole new opportunity for me at IBM. After helping Max and realizing how great the needs were, I went to management at IBM and presented my ideas. They were sold, and soon I had a technology lab in Southfield, Michigan, that I started for the purpose of designing equipment friendly to those with disabilities. Before long, IBM led the way in the corporate world in managing the needs of employees with disabilities. Ultimately, I began offering seminars to employers who were our customers about the needs facing those with disabilities. I called it "People Helping People through Technology."

In the midst of all this, in late June of 1991, Jenny and I adopted Will. He brought so much joy to our lives! Jenny took a leave from teaching with the intention of not going back. She was excited about being a stay-at-home mom and looking forward to the day when she could become involved in our son's schooling.

About six months after the adoption, IBM went through a reorganization. Until that time, no one in IBM had ever been laid off. The company became over-staffed in a changing market and this made layoffs inevitable. We were grateful the reorganization did not impact me. I still worked in the technology lab designing computer systems for the disabled.

In 1992, again the company had to downsize. IBM brought in outside help to obtain the goal of keeping as many people employed as possible. As Jenny and I prayed about this, we sensed the need to prepare for a layoff, just in case. During this new IBM reorganization, my job was still secure. Jenny still wanted to stay home with baby Will, and she also watched our nephew, Jon, and Elizabeth, the daughter of our good friends.

In mid-1993, IBM went through one more reorganization. This was at the same time I received the Disabled Computer Scientist of the Year Award. I flew back to Detroit on Friday morning and went into work Friday at noon. My boss, Phil, came over to my desk and asked to see me in his office. When he closed the door, he offered a sincere congratulation to me on my honorary award. "Larry," he said, "you really deserved that award; we are really happy for you!"

"Thank you, Phil," I responded.

Then Phil said, "Larry, I need to tell you that you no longer have a job at IBM. There have been severe cutbacks and your job was one of the first to go."

Talk about going from the heights of joy to the depths of sorrow in record time. There was no chance of being rehired. The company did not have the assets to keep benefits intact. "You have until July 1 to work here."

I had three months left at IBM. I felt stunned. I was concerned about the needs of the disabled after I was gone. "Lord," I inquired, "What do you want me to learn? What is it that you want to teach me?"

After seventeen years at the same job, it was difficult to take in all this change, but God seems to have a strange way of getting my attention at times. On occasions I did not put my trust in God and his provisions and my attitude became that of self-sufficiency in a prideful way. When I allowed pride to take control of my life, I would certainly find myself on the ground resulting from God's strong arm making an attitude adjustment. It is painful and puzzling, and it always provokes numerous questions in me.

Once I understand that I do not die after being knocked down, God's revelation of a bigger plan begins to unfold. 2 Corinthians 4:8-9 puts it this way: "We are hard pressed on every side, but not crushed; perplexed, but not in despair; persecuted, but not abandoned; struck down, but not destroyed."

There are trials we must endure so that we may be conformed to the image of Christ. The sooner we realize that this life is not about our pleasure, but rather God's glory, we find contentment no matter what storm may be raging in our existence. This scripture describes my experience while working hard to maintain a secure job at IBM.

As I left Phil's office, the emotional shock began wearing off, and I told the Lord, "If you can provide a family for Jenny and I the way you did, a job will be a piece of cake." I'm not sure if this was denial or faith. Little did I know how hard it would be letting go of my security blanket known as IBM, but God wanted to do so many things in my life, and so we began a new journey together as a family. If I was to grow and mature, the security blanket had to go.

The Lord gave us this scripture: "He tends his flock like a shepherd: He gathers the lambs in his arms and carries them close to his heart; he gently leads those that have young" (Isaiah 40:11).

I knew I had to let go of my security at IBM and give my fears to God. I really did not have a choice in the matter. It was God challenging me, saying, "Larry, I'm going to take away your security blanket. What will you do now?"

When God spoke to me through this scripture and challenged my heart, I realized that my relationship with him had grown distant. I didn't depend on Him so much anymore. Truly, I had become too comfortable and secure at IBM.

When I am speaking to an audience about this trial in my life, I use a powerful example of my son's stuffed animal Puffy. As Will grew out of babyhood and into a toddler, Puffy became part of the family. He went to bed with Will every night, worshipped in church every Sunday, and I don't know how many times Puffy has been to Florida.

But I knew that if I wanted my son to grow and mature, someday I might have to take Puffy away. This would be a hard day for both Will and me, but I didn't want to pay for an additional college education.

This example of Will and Puffy was exactly what God was doing for me. Not only does God want to provide for us, He wants to comfort us as well when things are tough.

After being laid off from IBM, the company made a very nice gesture toward the employees it had to let go. It paid for retraining programs, enabling greater chances for jobs out in the market. A six-week training program I had been trying to attend for four years called The Communication Project, a speaking and apologetics course through Campus Crusade for Christ, was being held at Colorado State University in Ft. Collins, Colorado.

This intense class focused on the skills used in public speaking and addressing audiences. Many facets of delivering the spoken word were explored and critiqued.

I left for this intense six-week training class the day after receiving my award and my layoff notification. Jenny flew out for a weekend after three weeks of being apart and we enjoyed being in Colorado together. It was difficult when she had to return home. I couldn't wait to finish the course and be home with my wife and little son.

Now that I was being laid off, I had to find work because ego would not take care of the bills. After I finished six weeks at The Communication Project, on August 1, 1993, I applied for a state level position modifying technology for the disabled. This job was right up my alley. When I walked into the interview for the position of Technology Specialist in the Lansing office, Jerry, one of my former IBM customers, was on the hiring board! I had helped him match a client with special needs equipment in January of 1991, so he knew me well and that my capabilities combined with my experience would make me a great candidate for the job.

Though I remained unemployed for six months before my new job began, God comforted my wife and me the whole time. I was very thankful for speaking engagements during this period, which provided a source of income for my family.

I began working for the state of Michigan in January, 1994, but six months of unemployment took its toll on our finances. We found it wise to rebuild our nest egg, so Jenny made the decision to go back to work. She got her third grade teaching position reinstated in the Royal Oak School district. This was a huge change in plans for Jenny, who had to give up her dream of being a stay-at-home mom.

After four years of working for the state, I was faced with a layoff again. Since Jenny had gone back to work full time to a job with full benefits, it was the perfect opportunity for me to step out and begin speaking full time.

I believe that if I had not been laid off from IBM, I would never have left to follow God's call to tell my story to audiences across the country. The process that the Lord brought me through to bring me into full-time ministry blows me away when I look back at it. I can see that what the Lord did was a good thing, despite the uncertainty and emotional pain I wrestled with.

I turned in my Bible to Psalm 71:19: "Your righteousness reaches to the skies, oh God, you who have done great things. Who, oh God, is like you?"

I developed a deep sense of wonderment in worshiping my Lord because of life's experience and taking God at his word.

After living through such trials God proved he was bigger than any obstacle in my life. My soul recognized that there is none like him. Who is like you Lord? Who can make beauty out of chaos? Who can take the loose strands of our lives and weave a rich tapestry covering the next generation? Who can take what was meant for evil and destruction and turn it to good? My answer is the Lord, because I see what he has done for me:

He took my twisted hands
And made them His very own,
He blessed my crooked feet
To reach the one alone,
He loosed my fettered tongue
For the work He had to do,
My broken body is His
That his healing might come to you.

9

Delivering a
Surprise Package

✳

*"For we are God's workmanship, created in
Christ Jesus to do good works, which God
prepared in advance for us to do."*

EPHESIANS 2:10

J enny, Will, and I had just returned from our February trip to
Colorado. Will was now almost nine and had become quite the
experienced skier. A week in Colorado was a yearly trip that our
family anticipated and enjoyed. We arrived home at 9:00 p.m.
Friday evening and Jenny was so exhausted that she headed right
for bed. I guess the traveling and high altitude in the mountains
took a toll on her this particular time.

While in Colorado, I had a fleeting idea to surprise Jenny
with a party for her fortieth birthday, but then I remembered
Jenny's expressed desire not to have a party. She began remind-
ing me when she turned thirty-five about not wanting a surprise.
Now that forty was around the corner, it became a weekly
reminder.

"Larry, I do not want a party!" she would say.

This all started when she turned twenty-nine and I surprised
her with a party. If you know me, you understand that I get the

biggest charge out of surprising people, especially my wife. I like surprises, so naturally, I assume Jenny will as well.

I had everything set up with my dad to bring her over to his house and everyone would shout "Surprise!" when she entered. To this day, I still do not know how she found out about her twenty-ninth birthday surprise party. Jenny refuses to incriminate her source.

Two days before the party, I was going out of town to speak. Before I left, she said she would see me Saturday evening. I knew exactly what she was referring to, because I would be home earlier Saturday afternoon and we would definitely see each other then. She didn't realize it, but she had just slipped knowing about her party!

This set me on a quest to really surprise her for her thirtieth birthday, especially since she made her wishes known after her twenty-ninth "surprise" that this was not what she wanted. Jenny didn't like the spotlight too much, but I figured I could cure her of that little problem. I decided to make it a real doozy next year! She was bound to love it, I thought.

So, almost a year later, I began making plans for Jenny's thirtieth. I secretly called some friends and family to fill them in on the surprise and to spread the word. Jenny's sisters handled some of the details so it could remain a surprise. Everything was set for the party to take place on March 27.

I told Jenny a few white lies; no, really I lied through my teeth! I had to get her there! I was having fun telling her falsehoods such as, "Let's go out to dinner at a nice quiet restaurant" and "Jenny, let's get a room for the night at the Marriott Courtyard across from the Palace in Auburn Hills."

I thought this would lure Jenny since we had been apart for two days. "Sounds relaxing," she said with a sigh.

There was a nice steak house out by the Palace, home of the Detroit Pistons, and we enjoyed a quiet evening together talking over tender prime rib. What Jenny did not know was that while we were dining, my brother Steve came to the restaurant parking lot and took the second hotel room key from under the floor mat on the driver's side of my car. Steve arranged a lookout point in the lobby of the hotel. At the proper time, the message would be relayed to the clerk at the desk, who would then phone our room to let thirty friends know we were on our way up.

When we finished our dessert, we, rather I, decided it was time to check into our room. At the desk, Jenny heard that we had a suite instead of a regular room. She insisted we didn't need a suite.

"Honey, doesn't that cost more money?" she demanded. "We don't need a suite, Larry. It's too much for one night!"

Now I had to think quickly. "Honey, it's the same price as a regular room on the weekend," I said, hoping she could not tell I was lying again.

After we reached our suite, I gave Jenny the key to open the door, after I had made a few farce attempts to get the card key into the lock system. When she opened the door, thirty voices shouted, "Surprise!"

I had so much fun watching her reaction! She was so stunned, it took her a good ten minutes to adjust to the shock of being surprised. The look on her face was priceless! After she caught her breath, Jenny managed to have a good time. Later that night when our guests had gone, we discovered they had short-sheeted our bed!

Now, several times a year for the next ten years, Jenny told me emphatically, "Nothing for my fortieth!"

So, coming home from our ski trip with her fortieth birthday right around the corner, she began telling me daily, "Nothing for my fortieth birthday, Larry. I really do not want a party!"

I could not understand why she did not want a party. I had been single for many years, so I obviously had a hard time reading my wife's love language. I finally resigned myself to loving her in the way she needed to be loved if I wanted our marriage to last. I also began to think more about this aspect of loving my wife. Did I want a party for her, or for myself? What would make her feel loved on her fortieth birthday?

I decided I would take her to dinner, and only dinner, just the two of us. As it turned out, Jenny could not go to dinner on her birthday because she was feeling poorly. It had been four to five weeks since we had come home from Colorado and Jenny was still very tired. She would come home from teaching and be so exhausted.

We decided we would wait until Friday evening the day after her birthday to celebrate, because she had a half-day and could take a nap before going out.

Jenny was concerned that she was not feeling well for so long. At first we thought it was the mountain air, but after being home for several weeks Jenny was still feeling fatigued.

She scheduled a doctor's appointment for late Friday afternoon, after school and before our dinner celebration.

Friday morning came and Jenny and I woke early for work and lingered around our bedroom for a few extra minutes talking. While making the bed together Jenny asked me, "Larry, do you think we should keep trying to adopt another child? I just turned forty yesterday and you will be forty-four. Will we be able to keep up?" I'm sure this was her fatigue speaking, but it got me thinking.

I sure liked that Will was older, and I liked going on trips and to soccer games. I enjoyed our lifestyle the way it was currently. I would soon be forty-four and that really would make it harder to keep up with a baby's needs. It would certainly change our lifestyle to adopt at this point.

"I'm not sure birth parents would choose us at our age," I answered while tucking in the comforter. Our decision was not set in stone, but we were moving in the direction of not pursuing another adoption. After getting ready, Jenny was leaving for school.

"Wait!" I said before she went out the door.

"Don't be late for your party," I teased. She stopped in her tracks.

"What party?" she demanded as she whirled around.

"Honey, I'm just kidding," I whispered to her before kissing her goodbye.

"That's the way I wanted it," she said, putting her chin up in satisfaction.

Early that afternoon, Jenny came home after school to take a nap. When I came into the bedroom several hours later I found Jenny still asleep on the bed. "She should be gone by now. Her appointment is at 3:45 p.m.," I said to myself, so I gently woke her.

I will never forget what happened when she came home at 5:30. I was there waiting to take her out to dinner. I had been so worried about Jenny. I knew she hadn't been feeling well, but this was taking much longer than I'd expected. Her doctor usually gets her in and out so quickly. By now I was getting hungry.

Moments later she came in the door and put her sweater and purse on the couch in the den. She did not say much, so I asked how her appointment went.

"Larry, you will not believe this," she said. "I am pregnant!"

I could not believe my ears. I felt like I was spinning out of control so I leaned against the back of my chair for support. "Say that again, Jenny. You're what?"

"Larry, I'm pregnant!

"Now I know why you've been so tired! I was so worried about you! Wait a minute," I said trying to process what Jenny had just repeated. "What about our infertility? How did this happen?" A flood of questions began tumbling out of my mouth.

" I am worried!" Jenny said. "Pregnant at forty!"

After a few minutes went by, I began to laugh because something about this was so hilarious. "You know how much I love

surprises! Well, I wanted to surprise you, Jenny, for your fortieth birthday. Did it work?"

"Yeah, I would say this tops all of the surprises over the years
put together!" she replied. She was not laughing at what I
thought was so funny. I got up from my recliner, walked over to
my wife who was still standing in the same place in shock, and
wrapped my arms around her. I leaned toward her and gently
kissed my wife, who was carrying our precious child inside of
her.

Two weeks later we were at the ultrasound appointment and
saw a tiny baby girl kicking and sucking her thumb inside Jenny's
womb. She looked so cute on the screen. As I saw her movements captured by ultrasound I was overwhelmed with emotion
and I couldn't keep it inside. The tears flowed as I looked down
at my lovely wife lying on the bed. I took her hand in mine and
kissed it softly.

When Jenny looked up at me she saw my joy, surprise, and
wonder at what God had given us. The ultrasound revealed that
our baby girl had secretly been with us for seventeen weeks. I
was so excited after the ultrasound that the following day I visited a woman's Bible study that consisted of women from our
Christian Marrieds group, telling them the news of our baby on
the way.

The more I told people about our news, the reality of being
forty-four and my wife being forty with a baby on the way
began to sink in. Jenny had been feeling very emotional and
now I was. But the more I talked to friends, the more I began to
see that God does not make mistakes.

I was reminded of Abraham and Sarah, well into their
nineties and having their first born child together. It may seem
funny, but my acceptance of a late-in-life pregnancy came just by
knowing I was less than half the age of Abraham. I figured, if he
can be a dad at his age, I can be a dad to my new baby at my age
with the help of God.

The remainder of Jenny's pregnancy was difficult. She developed gestational diabetes and the baby was continually in a breech position. The positioning of the baby was not critical until it became closer to delivery. The doctor kept a very close watch on Jenny and the baby through the rest of her pregnancy.

Five weeks before we had our daughter, Jenny's dad suddenly died of a heart attack early in the morning. This was a tremendous shock for Jenny, Will, and I. Somehow we made it through the next several weeks as we grieved the loss of her dad. He was so happy that we were going to have a baby. Now we would only have memories of him to share with our baby girl yet to come.

I tried to be the best labor coach I could possibly be. Every night I lay on the floor with Jenny and practiced labor massage, breathing exercises, and relaxation techniques. About three weeks before the birth we went in for a prenatal check. Our baby was still breech. The doctor was becoming concerned. He prepared us for a Caesarean birth just in case our daughter did not move into the head down position.

A friend of Jenny's told her to prop a board up against the headboard of the bed and extending down onto the mattress. She said if you lie on your back with your head at the bottom and feet toward the top of the board, it makes the baby want to flip into the correct position. Jenny did this for a few days and our little girl did it! She moved into the head down position.

Because of the gestational diabetes, the doctor wanted to induce labor. Babies born from mothers who have gestational diabetes are usually much larger than normal and this could cause problems for the newborn.

It was September 4 when the doctor admitted Jenny into the labor/delivery floor of Beaumont Hospital in Royal Oak, Michigan. Jenny was experiencing mild contractions already. The doctor seemed to think that inducement would be best after a good night's sleep, so he scheduled it for 9:00 a.m.

All night long Jenny could faintly hear the women who were laboring. She was somewhat frightened by the noise she heard because she had never experienced this before. Jenny wanted me to go home and sleep there so I could be with Will and return well rested in the morning. Nine o'clock came very early for me. I had a hard time getting to sleep after leaving Jenny at the hospital. I took Will to his cousin's house where he would stay with Aunt Julianne until after the baby was born.

When I came into Jenny's room, the nurse was adjusting the pitocin in her IV, a hormone used to stimulate labor. Jenny's labor progressed steadily. Her water broke at ten a.m., and I started rubbing Jenny's back because she indicated this was where she felt most of the labor.

Our little baby girl was posterior in position. This meant that her face was not against the inside of the pelvis but was opposite, with the back of her head riding down the inside of the pelvis. This can be very uncomfortable for a woman who is laboring.

By now it was after 12:00 p.m. The nurse told me this would be the best time to get something to eat, but I decided to wait. I didn't want to leave Jenny.

At 3:00 p.m. the nurse assured me I still had plenty of time to get a bite to eat. It was hard to know what to do. None of the birthing classes had prepared me for what I would feel emotionally. I went to the cafeteria and had a light dinner. When I returned back upstairs forty-five minutes later, the staff was busy putting a fetal monitor on Jenny. I walked into what seemed like chaos.

"What's happening?" I asked, seeing all of the commotion. The doctor was sitting on the bed checking the baby's heart rate by Doppler.

"Mr. Patton, the baby's heart rate began to drop drastically. We are putting the monitor on to keep a continuous watch on the heart rate. If the heart beat continues to drop under the

stress of contractions, we may be faced with having to do a Caesarean birth."

I was struggling to take in all of this new information.
Jenny's doctor was well aware of my worries because of what I
had experienced during my birth.

"How could so much happen in just forty-five minutes?" I
wondered. Jenny was now pushing and the doctor decided to try
forceps before resorting to a c-section. The doctor had a surgical
unit waiting just in case a forceps delivery was not going to
work. Jenny was lying on the bed, doing everything the doctor
instructed her to do.

"Jenny," the doctor said forcefully, "you have to push the baby
out now with each contraction!" I watched my wife in pain, I
held her hand, I told her she could do it, but inside I was not sure
if I could be the support she needed for this task. I glanced up at
the clock and it read 5:00 p m

I sat down in a chair next to Jenny's left side. I began the
counting as she pushed through another contraction. "1,2,3,4,5
. . . 10. Now breathe, Jenny," I instructed. The doctor worked to
get just the right set of forceps. The umbilical cord was being
compressed around one shoulder and under the arm of the baby,
which is why her heart rate was dropping.

"The baby is in distress," I heard him say to his nurses. "We
need to get the baby now!" The doctor reached for a suction forceps to deliver the baby. I was so frightened by the sound of all
of this. I kept praying the baby would be safe. I thought at that
moment about what my mother had experienced during my
delivery. I did not want this for my baby daughter.

I began praying like I never had before. "Please Lord, keep
her safe. Give Jenny the strength to deliver quickly!"

At 5:10 p.m. on Tuesday, September 5, 2000, Anna Lee Patton was born. She was twenty-one and a half inches long and
weighed eight pounds one ounce, and she was beautiful. No
c-section was required. The doctor gave me a pair of scissors to

cut the umbilical cord. He guided my hand's uncontrolled movement toward the area of where the cord should be cut. Then he said, "Go ahead, Larry."

This was one moment I will never forget. All of the stress of the delivery evaporated when I saw my tiny daughter. I noticed she had soft wisps of sandy hair as the team of nurses wiped her tiny head. Her little fingers and toes were scrunched up tightly and baby Anna drew her little knees up to her tummy. Her arms and legs were moving about as if trying to find mommy.

My daughter began to cry beautifully when the doctor listened to her heart with a tiny stethoscope. As the nurse placed Anna in Jenny's arms, I was looking at a miracle. Jenny's doctor could not explain why she had conceived but we knew why: the Lord had in mind to bless us with these children.

As Jenny stroked Anna's sweet little face, I leaned over the rail of the delivery bed to kiss Jenny's cheek. She was glowing and had never looked so beautiful to me.

What my wife endured to birth my daughter brought tears to my eyes. I sat down in the rocking chair by the window before the nurse placed Anna in my arms. While holding my precious baby girl, marveling at her existence, I asked Jenny teasingly, "What do you want for your fiftieth birthday?" At the time Jenny did not find my question very funny.

I took a quick moment to make a few calls to tell our good news. The first call I made was to my dad. I wanted to ask him to bring Will up to see Anna and Jenny. I picked up the phone to make the announcement when suddenly I felt waves of emotion wash over me. It was all happening so fast that it was difficult to understand just what I was feeling.

When Dad answered the phone, I froze for a moment and then began bawling. I must have managed to get words out that were somewhat intelligible because Dad understood it was me on the other end of the line. I wasn't just crying tears, I was bawling hard.

Because of my emotional reaction, my dad was afraid something was wrong. I struggled to get the news out while having such an emotional release. I began telling my dad the details of the cord wrapped around Anna, cutting off her oxygen supply. Through much emotion I was able to tell my dad how intense Anna's delivery was. He was quiet and just listened to the details unfold. "Dad, she is doing fine!" I said, trying to keep myself from crying.

When my dad finally understood that Jenny and baby Anna were doing well, he was filled with a sense of relief. He told me later that his mind was flooded with many memories of my first hours after birth as I told him about Anna's birth.

"Praise be to God!" he said, "For a safe delivery for your daughter and Jenny!" Dad was a man who didn't waste words. He said what he meant and really did not speak unless he intended to.

Before we hung up the phone, my father said to me one thing, in a way only my father could. "Everything will be fine now son, just fine." I began to weep again when I heard these words from him because my father understood my heart.

I knew all was fine, and that is why I cried so hard.

Now, every time I have a speaking engagement, I tell what God has done for us. Interestingly enough, Anna's name means "full of grace," and that is just what God has given to us.

10

Running for the Prize

✳

*"Therefore, since we are surrounded by such a great
cloud of witnesses, let us throw off everything that
hinders and the sin that so easily entangles, and let us
run with perseverance the race marked out for us. Let us
fix our eyes on Jesus, the author and perfector of
our faith, who for the joy set before him endured the
cross, scorning its shame, and sat down at the
right hand of the throne of God."*

HEBREWS 12:1-2

*"I really don't have goals to be the greatest coach in the
business. I just try to achieve the best with the talents
God has given me. If I do that, I'm satisfied."*

COACH TOM LANDRY

On a cold rainy day in April, 1996, I was home from work
recovering from a fall. My elbow was inflamed and I needed to
rest it. The phone rang. I picked it up to hear a man's voice.

"Hello, Larry? My name is Harry Krupsky and I am the minister of Family Life at Faith Lutheran Church in Troy. I heard
about your speaking ministry, Hurdling Handicaps, and would
like more information." Harry invited me to lunch so we could

discuss the possibility of me speaking at the men's retreat in the fall.

We met in a little restaurant in Berkley for lunch the next day. I checked out the dates with my ministry coordinator, Lori Thomas, and the dates were available so we booked the retreat.

Harry was a very kind and gentle-natured man. He had been serving as Family Life Minister at Faith Lutheran since 1981. He has been a great blessing to many in the church by offering resources, counseling, and prayer.

At our first meeting he encouraged me greatly in my ministry. We enjoyed the rest of our lunch together, discussing different aspects of ministry.

In October, I spoke to the group of men from Faith Lutheran Church. I walked up to the podium and before I began to speak into the microphone, I took a look around the room. I saw a few men looking at my disability, not at me.

I had learned to move through the awkwardness of an audience to talk about God's life-changing power. Whenever I sensed doubt about my ability from an audience, this was when the Lord worked mightily. I wanted to show them that the ability in my disability came from God, that it was Christ in me.

I offered up a flare prayer. That is what I call a prayer that needs to be said in a hurry when there is no time for a long one. When I opened my mouth to speak, I did not plan my words in advance like I usually did.

I started out by asking, "Have you ever prayed for something with all of your heart? Did you hear 'No' from God? Was the answer 'No' hard to accept? That has been my life story. Thankfully, I did receive the grace to accept God's 'No' for an answer, and all he had in store for my life."

The Lord showed me what to say next.

"It was really tough growing up on the playground. The other children didn't know what to do with me. When I played ball with the rest of them, or climbed on the monkey bars, the kids eventually got to know me. I didn't apologize for who I was, or for my twisted body. The other kids soon found that I wasn't so scary after all."

I could see defenses dropping. I continued, "Everyone is handicapped in some way. The only difference is, you can see mine." Now I could see that they were ready to listen to what the Lord had to say through me.

I told my life story. I told how my mother prayed for my life to be spared at birth, and how she blazed a trail that shaped my whole life. Then I spoke about my desire to be healed.

"Have you ever prayed about something with all of your heart? I started to pray about being healed when I was a young teenager experiencing God's love in Jesus Christ for the first time. I was always told of God's love, but now I was experiencing it for myself. I reasoned that if God loved me, he would heal me. I prayed with all of my heart to a God of love; surely he would heal my prayers and heal me.

"I trusted God to perform a miracle, but God's answer always seemed to be 'No.' When I went to the Holy Land, I received peace and accepted for the first time 'No' as his answer. Before this time, I did not want to believe the answer was 'No.' It seemed as though I was living an unanswered prayer."

I could see the Lord reaching men through this contorted body and the voice God had provided for me.

Harry Krupsky heard me speak at this retreat and was very intrigued. He later said it caused him to read *More Than an Average Guy*, a book about my life. The more Harry read, the more he wanted to get to know me.

Shortly after I spoke at the retreat, my mother fell ill. She had been struggling with Parkinson's syndrome for a few years. Seeing my mom so ill was very difficult for me. She had been a driving force in my ability to overcome my disability. My mother, Sue Patton, dedicated herself to me for the first eighteen years of my life, helping me make a way for myself in this world.

She slipped into a coma the Friday after Thanksgiving in 1996. As I visited her in the critical care unit, my heart ached inside and I told her how much I loved her and thanked her for all of her love and care for me. I understood how much she had sacrificed.

In early December of that year, my father made the decision to take her off of life support upon receiving the news that she was now brain dead. When she was extubated, we thought she would pass on quickly. No one could explain why, but she lived another five weeks. My father, Steve, and I spent every waking moment at the hospital. We cried together and remembered all the wonderful blessings of her life.

Watching my mother slip away was one of the most difficult times in my life. She took her last breath on January 1, 1997, and many months of intense grieving followed for my Dad, Steve, me, and our families. Will was now five years old. I knew he was old enough to understand what happens to people when they die.

I sat Will down in our living room to tell him the news. I asked my son if he knew where Jesus lived. Will's five-year-old answer was not what I expected. "Right here, in my heart," he said, as he placed his hand on his little chest.

I said, "You're right, Will! Jesus does live in your heart. He did a very special thing for Grandma Patton today. He took her to live in Heaven, so she can live with Him forever." Will accepted this with all sincerity.

Later that month, Jenny and I made a commitment to become members of Faith Lutheran Church. Harry and many others had been a great support to us after my mother passed away. We already knew a few couples who worshipped there, and in fact, one couple who knew of our quandary over where to worship had suggested we come with them to church one Sunday.

When we took them up on the offer, we knew right away we had found our church home. This was an answer to our prayer. We had waited so long to know where God would lead us. Indeed, this struggle had been ongoing since I proposed to Jenny in 1986. We were glad to finally have our "where to worship" problem resolved, but it had taken nine years and Will was now six years old—so much for not having a family until our place of worship was decided!

In August of 1997 we moved closer to church after finding a beautiful brick ranch home in Troy. We felt truly settled after making this move and becoming members of Faith Lutheran Church.

In 1999 I came across a great resource concerning my speaking ministry when I became a member of the National Speakers Association (NSA). Since this group is comprised of men and woman from all walks of life and many different backgrounds, I found it to be a wonderful way to polish my presentations.

The N.S.A. experience could be summed up as "People helping people."

When I first heard about the meetings, I thought it would be an organization with a competitive nature. After all, everyone was competing for the same dollars out there, but it really was not that way at all. Everyone has his or her own audience to speak to and no two people have the exact same market. Amazing! Jenny and I went together to my first conference in San Antonio.

At lunchtime we grabbed our boxed lunches and went to the patio of the hotel to eat. We had thirty minutes before we needed to be back inside where the meeting was held. We met a nice couple on the patio over lunch. During our conversation we found out that we were all Christians. John and Juanita asked us, "Do you know about the prayer meeting tonight?"

Jenny and I looked at each other excitedly. "No," we replied.

"We gather together to pray that we can really be used by the Lord to reach people for Christ," Juanita continued.

There we were, in a meeting room at a hotel full of Christian speakers that night. We felt blessed to meet so many Christians in the same business. We even got to meet the vice president of the National Speakers Association. When we left to go home a few days later, we knew God was beginning to open new doors for speaking.

Jenny and I spent more time talking with Harry Krupsky later that year. The more he found out about us, the more he thought I would be a good fit with Men's Ministry.

As it turned out, in June of 2000, two and a half years after Jenny's and my membership commitment to Faith Lutheran, a part-time staff position opened up for Men's Ministry. Harry could not coordinate all the Men's Ministry events plus keep all the ministries under Family Life in order, so he asked to have a man hired who could take on the Men's Ministry responsibilities for the church, thus freeing him up to oversee the Family Life ministries.

Harry also made it known that he had just the guy for the job, a man who had been involved voluntarily for three years. He had gotten to know me very well over these few years and had watched me never give up, encourage others, and awaken people to reach for the hopes and dreams God had placed in their hearts. Faith Lutheran Church hired me, and I began as a part-time staff member on July 1, 2000.

My job was and remains a true blessing. I serve on staff at the church, ministering to men. The position is a perfect fit for me, and the staff at Faith Lutheran is supportive of my speaking ministry, Hurdling Handicaps. I am encouraged to grow my ministry and use it to God's glory.

Unbeknownst to me, in 2001, Harry heard about General Motors sponsoring the Olympic Torch run across the United

States. The advertisement included information on how to nominate special persons to help carry the Olympic Flame before the 2002 Winter games. Harry nominated me, and I was chosen to do a run.

When I found out I had received the privilege of carrying the flame, I was awestruck. I questioned, "Why should I carry the flame?" The Lord showed me right there that he wanted to use me in this twisted body to be a light that shines in the darkness to the glory of God!

Thus, on that cold dark winter night of January 6, 2002, I found myself boarding a bus with eleven other strangers. These strangers consisted of a hockey player, a police officer, a mother, a fireman, a father and daughter team, an automotive executive, a secretary, a TV newscaster, and me, a professional speaker. Each of us, everyday Americans, had been individually selected to take part in this very special event.

After traveling a few miles, we were dropped off at our assigned locations along Woodward Avenue in Highland Park, Michigan.

Over one hundred family members and friends began cheering as I stepped off the bus that night into the cold. I was full of emotions and expectations.

Within three to four minutes of stepping off the bus, I looked up and saw the Olympic Flame burning brightly in the darkness coming right toward me. Then I was holding my Olympic Torch high in the night air, preparing to receive the Olympic Flame. As my torch lit, I realized I was the only one in the world to be holding and carrying the Olympic Flame.

That flame had been lit on November 19, 2001, in Olympia, Greece. Once ignited, the flame had been kept in a lantern that accompanied the torch relay covering more than 13,500 miles across America, through forty-six states in sixty-five days.

The torch relay finished in Salt Lake City on February 8, 2002, marking the beginning of the nineteenth Winter Olympic Games.

I turned and began running my two-tenths of a mile segment of the Olympic Torch Relay with cheering spectators lining the city street to catch a view of the Olympic Flame and to encourage me along each step of the way.

What a great privilege and honor to be carrying the Olympic Flame! For me, it was a thrill of a lifetime to play a small role in the Winter Olympic Games, but even a greater privilege is to tell why this light burns so brightly inside me.

All my life, I will tell of the love of God and what Jesus did for each of us on the cross as long as I have breath. If my twisted body is a light to the world, then I choose to be the light of Christ shining in the darkness.

Epilogue

*"God is a specialist at making something useful
and beautiful out of something broken and confused."*

CHUCK SWINDOLL

Running past the crowd with exhilaration in the air was an experience I will never forget. Here on Woodward Avenue as I ran, all the pieces of my life began to fit together like a puzzle, making an incredible word picture of God's saving grace, mercy, and love.

Running with the torch, my thoughts drifted back to the life events that had so painfully and beautifully shaped and molded my life. I felt the strength of God carrying my ravaged body through my two-tenths of a mile stretch down Woodward Avenue.

Never before had I run as I did that night. I experienced God saying, "I am going to use you in ways you have not dreamed possible. My glory will be seen in you, and many will come to know that I live, and purchased each life with the price of my beloved Son. Tell all those you meet about the love of your God."

This was an incredible moment for me. The sleet coming down from the dark clouds above could not dampen the emotion I felt that night. The wind could not blow the Spirit of God away, and the cheers from the crowd could not drown out the soft still voice of my Lord speaking to me.

When I saw my wife Jenny in the crowd with her head bowed, praying for me, I felt so connected to her and I recognized this as truly a gift from God. When she looked up, our eyes met for a brief moment as I ran past. I saw so much love and support in her eyes.

Standing next to Jenny was our son Will. I thought about the father-son ski trip to Colorado we would be taking together in a few short weeks. Then I saw Anna, our sweet baby daughter, being passed to mommy from Aunt Chris.

"Lord, you are the potter and I am the clay." Life is so much more when we realize that we are the clay to be molded and shaped by the potter, a vessel used for His purpose to glorify him. When we can grab hold of this, life somehow has meaning and fulfillment.

✳

A few weeks passed after the torch run, and it was time for our annual ski trip to Snowmass, Colorado. It was going to be a very different week than usual. Jenny would stay home with our daughter Anna, and Will and I would make it a father and son ski trip.

We always took this trip during winter break from school in February, and we had looked forward to it with much anticipation ever since Will had learned to ski. This year, Will was looking forward to trying new and more difficult slopes. He had grown a great deal over the last year, which gave him a boost in confidence.

The chairlift was coasting us into position at the top of the mountain. Before getting off the lift, I turned to Will, quickly reviewing a few points. Taking special effort to enunciate clearly through my impaired speech, I began telling him, "You may wipe out a few times, but the sooner you get up the better. I know this is review for you, son, but don't think you know it all. Learn to review the basics . . . after all, this is a blue diamond slope."

Looking down the steep mountain, fresh with light fluffy powder and a brisk Colorado wind, Will swallowed hard. His quick eye motion said to me, "I think I can do this!"

"Will, I'll be right with you all the way," I responded.

First Will started down the mountain, and I followed closely behind him. I weaved the slopes effortlessly, as though no disability existed. The freedom I felt was only enhanced as I used my body movements to steer and direct my path. This is why I do not use poles when I ski. No poles means, nothing to inhibit my momentary freedom from the ravages of cerebral palsy.

As Will picked up speed, accuracy, and confidence, he shouted, "Dad, this is fun!" and with a jerky hand motion, I encouraged my son onward.

"Lord, I am so blessed to be here with my son. What a gift he is to us! Thank you for a perfect way to spend a mid-winter break, bringing us here to Snowmass."

Learning to ski was such a thrill for my son. He watches me learn the meaning of thrill and victory almost daily, so he knows that taking on a new challenge means growth

"I'm so proud of you, Will!" The words of encouragement came bursting from my mouth as we reached the bottom of the slope. "When I learned to ski I fell all the time."

Will was encouraged by this old news, even though he didn't fall much. He knew persistence was a lesson worth learning, especially from dad. As a dad, I always try to impress on Will's heart the truths God will place before him. These are lessons of patience, persistence, focus, and grace.

Now, with our last day upon us, I was amazed at how quickly our time had flown. "Son, remember what it looked like out here just four days ago?"

Will answered, "Yeah, I remember! It was snowing and foggy and too cold for me."

"We couldn't see the slopes really at all," I reminded. "I fell more than twelve times that one day alone! And I am so grateful that you were such a good sport about helping me up!" As I took a deep breath of clean crisp air, I took in the complete contrast in weather from four days ago.

"Look what we have today, Will! It's so clear! Not a cloud in the sky." The conditions were perfect. The snow was clean and fresh, and the sky was clear as far as the eye could see. "We just finished our time out here with that beautiful run, and you know? I only fell three times over the last three days combined!"

Will responded with a grin, "Yeah, a big improvement from four days ago!"

I was standing off to Will's right. Picking up on the sense of humor in his remark, I slapped my left gloved hand against the back of his right shoulder. Will looked up at me, rolling his head back in laughter. A friendly wink from me sealed the moment.

✳

Will turned his attention to removing his skis and cleaning off the fresh snow. In the process of cleaning off his skis, he looked up at me. Recognizing the expression on my face, he knew another truth was about to emerge.

"This reminds me of carrying the Olympic Flame in January." A sense of enlightenment filled me. "I see it like this . . . I carried that torch lit with the Olympic Flame. It was dark outside, but I could see far enough ahead of me because of the light the torch gave.

"The truth is, if we are Christians, we all have a lighted torch inside burning brightly; it is the light of Christ. When we have His light inside of us, shining on our path, even with imperfections and problems, we can see more clearly, just like on the slopes today. We may fall down because we live in a fallen world, but it won't be as hard or as often. We need to share our flame with others, to let them know what God is doing in our lives. If Christ is trusted as Savior, then He will be present; He will guide us, and catch us when we fall. God keeps his promises."

Will listened as I spoke and understood as best as a ten-year-old boy could. One thing Will did understand clearly is that life offers opportunities to learn and grow, and how we respond to life's challenges is important. Will these challenges turn us to Christ, or harden our hearts?

As Will and I headed toward the hotel shuttle for the last time, skis over our shoulders, I was feeling so blessed to have spent this time with my son. It never could have happened if a few of my friends hadn't sacrificed their time and energy teaching me. Skiing had become something Will and I looked forward to doing together. I thanked God for friends who believed in me because I now had a gift, a talent I could share with my son.

When we got back to the hotel room, Will and I began packing to leave on an early morning flight back home to Michigan. We recounted the events and highlights of each day spent in Colorado while tossing our belongings into our suitcases, basketball style. Upon finishing our task, I tucked Will into his bed and told him how glad I was that we had come.

"Me, too," Will responded through a hearty yawn.

"Go to sleep now, Will. Morning will come very soon!" I pulled the comforter up around Will and blessed him as he nestled into his bed. As I crawled into the other bed, reviewing in my mind the days we had spent skiing, I reached to turn out the light. My thoughts related skiing to our walk with Christ.

"A life in Christ gives us the light we need to live in this world, all the while knowing we are really citizens of Heaven. We would never ski in the dark, especially on the mountain slopes we were just on, nor would we go beyond the markers."

It made a shiver run down my spine to think about falling down the side of a mountain. God gives us boundaries to protect us. Danger would be certain if we veered off the path. Proverbs says that God's word is a lamp for our feet and a light to our path. I know it is His desire that we spend eternity with him.

I thought about all the people on the slopes that dreadful, foggy day a few days before. If a skier decided not to follow the path or perhaps lost his way and went beyond the markers, it would mean falling down the side of the mountain to certain death.

I wondered, "Where would this person spend eternity?" I thought about those who cross my path who are headed for the side of the mountain.

Am I telling them of the saving knowledge of Jesus Christ or letting them fall to their deaths? Am I telling them that Jesus came in the flesh to show us He understands our human condition? Am I telling them that he was born of a virgin, grew to be a man, and was perfect, without sin?

I need to tell that Jesus took our sin upon Himself, on the cross. I need to tell that he died a torturous death in our place. I need to tell that he was buried, and then on the third day he rose from the dead, conquering sin and death. Through Jesus Christ, we can live eternally in Heaven with God the Father. What freedom we can know if we trust Jesus Christ as our Savior!

As I lay in the dark, I thought about the freedom I experience when I ski. This is the only time I feel graceful and in control of my body. For a brief moment, I am free from the effects cerebral palsy has on me. I weave effortlessly down the slopes, gliding through all the twists and bends. It makes me think how wonderful it is being set free from sin. Some may say I am crazy to do such a thing as downhill skiing with my disability, but I think it mirrors faith.

Faith is hard to practice, just as skiing was in the beginning for me. Once faith begins to grow, it increases in measure, always producing new opportunities to stretch and grow, knowing deeper the freedom in Jesus Christ. To live by faith is exhilarating! It is exciting, just like skiing down the slope of a mountain.

My eyes were getting heavier with sleep, but I managed one more series of thoughts. "We can move through life with the help of other Christians. Sometimes we just need a hand up when we fall down; at other times it may be that we need someone along

side to encourage us to keep going, or perhaps we need someone who knows the way through the foggy path to keep us from
danger.

"When we recognize the gifts in the body of Christ, we can
help and encourage each other on the long, difficult, and winding path of life. When I hear people say that they have a relationship with Christ but do not need church, it breaks my heart. All
of us in Christ are part of his body. We need the hands, the feet,
the eyes, the heart, and all parts to be complete. Living in a body
that is disabled, I can see how important it is not to handicap the
body of Christ."

There were so many thoughts running through my mind
about being out on the slopes. I had learned so much being out
there. Sleep was coming to me now after a long day.

My thoughts drifted to home. I was ready to see Jenny and
Anna. I wondered how much my baby girl had grown in one
week. I turned my sleepy gaze toward the window. The dark
room gave way to the reflecting snow outside. It cast a dim light
through the curtains, giving the room a faint hint of illumina-
tion.

I looked over at Will, already asleep in his cozy bed, and I
studied his face in the dim light. "He is getting so big," I thought,
trying to keep my eyes from giving in to sleep. Through a muffled
yawn, I whispered, "Good night, Will," then I drifted off to sleep.

More than an average Guy
about Larry Patton